Reserve Stock

Telephone : 01 - 340 3343

HIGHGATE LITERARY & SCIENTIFIC
INSTITUTION
II, SOUTH GROVE, N.6

428 How

14672

Time allowed FOURTEEN Days

Date Issued	Date Issued	Date Issued
3 OCT 1977	9 JAN 1978	
1 1 OCT 1977	6 FEB 1979	
5 NOV 1977	2 4 FEB 1979	
2 4 NOV 1977	3 0 MAR 1979	
1 0 APR 1978	2 6 APR 1979	
	2 3 JUN 1979	
6 MAY 1978	5 OCT 1979	
6 JUN 1978	1 4 NOV 1979	
2 0 JUL 1978	6 DEC 1979	
	1 4 FEB 1981	
1 0 AUG 1978	2 9 AUG 1985	
2 8 OCT 1978		
1 8 NOV 1978		
2 5 NOV 1978		
2 0 DEC 1978		

NEW WORDS FOR OLD

PHILIP HOWARD

New Words for Old

HAMISH HAMILTON
LONDON

First published in Great Britain 1977
by Hamish Hamilton Ltd
90 Great Russell Street London WC1B 3PT

Copyright © 1977 by Philip Howard

SBN 241 89722 x

Printed in Great Britain by
Bristol Typesetting Co Ltd
Barton Manor St Philips Bristol

14672
────────
428

For Jamie

CONTENTS

INTRODUCTION

In a living language all is flux, nothing is stationary. For prescriptive grammarians the only good languages are dead ones. The vocabularies and grammars of classical Greek and Latin are almost complete. Occasionally a brave new word turns up from an Oxyrhyncus papyrus or some other still-trickling source. Occasionally a classical scholar produces a persuasive emendation or new interpretation that has eluded the collective wisdom of textual critics of the past twenty centuries. Modern scholarship is at present particularly interested in ancient technology, and is producing far more accurate accounts of technical terms than have been available before. But, in general, ancient Greek and Latin are fixed and finite languages. When the final fascicle of the *Oxford Latin Dictionary* is published, probably in 1982, it will be the last word that needs to be said on the subject until the Last Trump, at which awful blast every crux shall be unravelled and the rough places and etymologies made plain.

This makes the classical languages ideal playgrounds for grammarians and ideal drill-yards for students of language. They have a precision and stability that is not available in a living language : the stability and constancy of the grave. Their syntax is preserved beneath the silence of the centuries as perfectly as the ruins of Pompeii beneath the killing layers of ash and pumice. So the prescriptive grammarian can make rules, and adjudicate magisterially that this is right, that is wrong, this goes in the subjunctive, that in the dative. He can lay down the law without fear of contradiction by vulgar new usages or anarchists who refuse to follow his rules. The fifth foot of a hexameter must be a dactyl not a spondee. Although Propertius (*Sunt apud infernos tot milia formosarum*) and Lucretius (*Insatiabiliter deflevimus, aeternumque*) broke this rule once or twice with majestic poetic effect, the modern student versifier will be marked wrong if he follows in their footsteps, unless he can persuade the examiner that he did so on purpose and to good effect.

Until the sixteenth century 'grammar' in English use meant mainly Latin grammar. Grammar schools were so called because they were founded for the teaching of Latin grammar. Until quite recently it was supposed that English grammar ought to behave like Latin, conforming to fixed rules that enabled one to judge that certain constructions and meanings for words were correct English, and certain others were incorrect. Thus Lowth in the introduction to his *Grammar* of 1762 wrote of rules 'by the observing of which you will avoid mistakes'.

The old certainties were founded upon shifting sand, and their ruin has been great. Prescription is out of fashion in language as in many other activities. We no longer believe in mistakes. Schools no longer teach English grammar or try to stretch or mutilate English to conform to a Procrustean bed of correctitude. We have recognized that language is a functional instrument for conveying meanings, and that English is the queen of languages because of its flexibility, adaptiveness, and freedom from rules. Even the great Dr Johnson was not so lost in lexicography as to forget that words are the daughters of earth, and that things are the sons of heaven.

English is a rich and restless ocean that absorbs and is strengthened by words and usages from every other language that has flowed from the Tower of Babel. From Russian it has adopted dozens of loanwords from vodka (the diminutive of *vodá*, water) to samizdat. When Soviet space scientists launched their first sputnik in 1957, they launched simultaneously a vogue suffix into the English language that flourishes in such words as peacenik and beatnik (the latter has recrossed the Atlantic and the Iron Curtain as *bitnik* to re-enter the Russian language in its own right). Denis Healey has been aptly described as an intellectual roughnik. We borrowed extensively from Indian languages during the three and a half centuries of our extraordinary imperial connexion: pundit, thug, khaki, bungalow, jungle, and many other words that have become naturalized English without the faintest connotation of being exotic. We have been borrowing from French for so long that thousands of loanwords are quite at home, and have entirely lost their whiff of garlic and frenchified accents. Denim came from *serge de Nîmes* (the manufacturing town and capital of the Gard Department in the South of France) in the seventeenth century. Jeans got their name as early as the sixteenth century from the material manufactured at *Gênes*, the French name for Genoa. Poplin is dubiously held to come from *papeline* (Italian *papalina*), because it was made at Avignon, the French papal town.

And now Malayan, Australian, West Indian, Japanese, and the other languages from the round earth's imagined corners are adding tributaries year by year to flow into the diverse richness and inexhaustible variety of the English ocean. North America is by far the richest and most imaginative source of new English, while at the same time being the most fecund source of ugly and deleterious words and usages. The great linguistic melting pot is bound to produce scum as well as new metals.

We have learned to welcome the constant flux and growth of English less grudgingly than Dr Johnson, who wrote in the preface to his *Dictionary of the English Language*: 'If the changes that we fear be thus irresistible, what remains but to acquiesce with silence, as in the other insurmountable distresses of humanity? It remains that we retard what we cannot repel, that we palliate what we cannot cure.'

Nevertheless, not all change is for the better in the best of all possible words. Some new words and new constructions are indeed mistaken and erroneous. Or, if those unfashionable epithets are considered too paternalistically prescriptive, they are harmful and inefficient because they reduce the precision of the language. For example, the common misuse of 'disinterested' as a bogus synonym for 'uninterested' adds nothing to the language, and erodes a useful meaning, which is not quite the same as 'unbiased'. The erosion of the subjunctive and the decline of the accusative cases of personal pronouns are blunting the language by reducing the available discriminations. Above all, the pernicious political dialect of Doublespeak or Newspeak, and its argots of PROspeak (the cant of the public relations industry) and Adspeak (the gibberish of the advertising industry), are intended to hoodwink the public, and progressively narrow the range of ideas and independent thought. They use lying words as contranomers to dupe rather than to enlighten and communicate.

The great *Oxford English Dictionary* in its old age is becoming more prescriptive about such linguistic frauds. The modern scientific idea of a dictionary is that it should describe the way that the language is actually used as objectively as possible, without passing judgments on the words it describes, to form a permanent record of the language. But volume two of the *OED Supplement, H-N,* published in 1976, takes a bolder line than its predecessors about condemning erroneous and offensive words. It describes 'miniscule', widely misapprehended to mean 'very small', as erroneous. It deprecates 'insinuendo', the portmanteau blending of insinuation and innuendo, as 'a tasteless word'. It condemns such racialist terms as 'nigger', 'honky', and 'to jew' (transitive verb) as contemptuous ethnic abuse and offensive.

Robert Burchfield, the chief editor of the Oxford English dictionaries and editor of the *OED Supplement,* has become increasingly concerned about the proliferation and fragmentation into compartments of the central core of English, which ought to be familiar to everyone who can be said to know the language. This fission is particularly prevalent in the central core of American English. Ethnic minorities in the United States tend to preserve the languages, accents, and idiosyncratic uses of the lands that their immigrant forefathers came from, and to campaign vigorously for these immigrant dialects to be brought into the educational system and officially recognized in other ways. Having their language accepted means jobs and money. As a consequence the central core of American English is breaking up into dialects, and becoming an increasingly unattractive model as a language for speakers at a distance. Even within the United States different communities and regions are finding it more and more difficult to understand each other.

Fortunately in Britain we manage to integrate our immigrants quite successfully, linguistically at any rate, with the result that a West Indian or Asian born and educated in this country speaks English with one of the native British accents, and uses words in their native senses. But with so many millions using English as their first or second language, with different dialects, vocabularies, and grammars in different parts of the world, there is a danger that the universal ocean of English may be split and parcelled into a number of mutually incomprehensible dialects.

The English language is an ocean in which elephants can swim and lambs can paddle. It belongs to all those who use it. The only guardians it has are self-appointed. But to prevent its pollution benefits all its users. Fortunately we have no organization like the Académie Française charged with the task of keeping the language pure by acting as linguistic censor to turn back undesirable alien words at the frontier: a duty as hopeless and ludicrously ill-conceived as Dame Partington trying to push back the Atlantic with her mop. There is an agreeable irony about journalists in particular setting themselves up as guardians of the Queen's English. Journalists, in company with other communicators of the mass media and ancillary industries, are principal culprits in the erosion of the language by imprecision, exaggeration, cliché, hazy use of popularized technicalities, overuse of modish words and phrases, and other such literary vices. They do it because of the hurry in which they usually have to write, and because of their old Athenian instinct either to tell or to hear some new thing. A proclivity to fashionable new words and recycled old clichés goes naturally with a preoccupation with the news.

Accordingly a journalist taking a high prescriptive line about correct English may seem to some as hypocritical and irritating a spectacle as Satan reproving sin. But at least he can plead (as Satan can) that by being exposed daily in his business to linguistic temptation and falling continually into linguistic sin, he knows temptation and sin more intimately than people in more sheltered occupations. A semantic poacher is well-equipped to set up as gamekeeper. His prescriptions are directed chiefly at himself, with a view to restraining his adjectives and other pleasant vices. They are not aimed *de haut en bas* at comparatively blameless users of English outside journalism, broadcasting, advertising, the social sciences, politics, and the other trades that abuse the language. They are penitential prescriptions *de profundis*.

The Times of London has a long and honourable tradition of being cautious about publishing new words with no references. Its style-book is sternly prescriptive about such matters as insisting on quantities of blood before a scene can be described as a shambles, and protesting that to scotch a snake or a rumour is not at all the same thing as killing it. It puts a new word on probation in inverted commas for a long time, sometimes for many years, before formally recognizing its entry into the language and removing them.

A journalist is in the best position to know that nothing excites readers of English more than a misprint or misuse of English. People feel threatened by change, particularly by change in something so personal as the language they were taught as children. Letters from vigilant readers flood in to point out in triumph, rage, or *schadenfreude* the tiniest literal or the most venial solecism in their daily newspaper. It is, in fact, astonishing how few there are, when it is considered that a morning newspaper does not start being written before noon at the earliest, and yet manages to present twice as many words as the average novel, nearly all of them correctly used and impeccably printed, on the breakfast tables of the nation the next morning. A journalist, who may have to write a thousand words in half an hour on an unfamiliar subject, with his news desk screaming for copy, with no time to read let alone revise what he has written, and with sub-editors snatching the copy sheet by sheet from his typewriter, should be excused an occasional lapse into solecism.

Nevertheless, precision of language is beneficial both to writer and to reader. The primary purpose of language is to convey meaning. There are already enough opportunities in the world for misunderstanding each other, without adding to them by attaching inexact or chameleon meanings to words, and so fouling the channels of communication.

The idea for these articles on changing words and meanings was conceived in the autumn of 1975. As she was removed forcibly from court, Ulrike Meinhof, the West German terrorist leader, shouted at her judge: 'You imperialist state-pig.' This remarkable insult caught the attention of William Rees-Mogg, the editor of *The Times,* a man with an interest in words by nature as well as *ex officio.* He wondered what Frau Meinhof could have had in mind. Most of these essays that grew from that original investigation have been published in *The Times.* They have all been revised, and many of them radically rewritten in the light of the correspondence that they provoked. One of the advantages of writing for *The Times* is that its readers are the most learned, witty, and persistent letter-writers in the epistolarian world. An unintentional libel on no less eminent personages than Sir Harold Wilson's press officers at Number Ten Downing Street has been removed, along with other less sensational and less expensive blemishes.

Anybody who attempts to write about words and meanings rides on the backs of the learned and patient tribe of lexicographers, especially those of the *Oxford English Dictionary,* that most informative and entertaining of all books. The Merriam-Webster *Webster's Third New International Dictionary* (1971) and its supplement, *6000 Words* (1976), are the most reliable authorities on American usage, being particularly good at selecting apt quotations that define as well as illustrate the words. Devilish Ambrose Bierce defined lexicographer, n., as: 'A pestilent fellow who, under the pretense of recording some particular stage in the development of a language, does what he can to arrest its growth, stiffen its flexi-
xiv

bility, and mechanize its methods.' This is a misunderstanding of what lexicographers are about. They chart the ocean, but are not concerned with deep-sea engineering or preventing environmental pollution. The living language evolves and changes because of the way that we all use it, just as the ocean changes its shape because of tides and currents, silt and erosion, and the massive, imperceptible movement of the continents. The marine cartographer is not to be held responsible for the changes he records. Any writer about words is head over heels in debt to all the dictionary-makers, from Funk and Wagnall and Chambers to Longman, the editor of whose *Modern English Dictionary*, Peter Owen, combines the delightful professions of lexicographer and potter, so doing more good and less harm to mankind than most men.

I thank Jimmy Greenwood, most punctilious of sub-editors, Jan Stephens, Margaret Allen, Don John, Michael Hamlyn, William Rees-Mogg, Bernard Levin, Louis Heren, and other colleagues on *The Times* for suggesting new words and arguing about what they mean.

I thank Dr John Apley, Clive Ashwin, Dr A. G. Atkins, Professor Denis Baron, Robert Burchfield, Ned Chaillet, Tom Christopher, the Hon. Sir David Croom-Johnson, the Rev. Dudley Davies, R. N. Dixey, Anne Donaldson, Neil Fisk, George Gale, Philip Hope-Wallace, Stephen Hugh-Jones, James Kirkup, Professor N. Kurti, D. M. Lewis, P. C. Macnamara, Charles Morris, James Ottaway, William Palmer, J. S. F. Parker, Isobel Raphael, Cyril Ray, S. C. Richardson, Professor Alan Ross, Arthur Seldon, Professor D. H. Smyth, John Sykes, Bryan Tassell, W. E. van Heyningen, Sir Anthony Wagner, Commander Charles Walker, Brian Walsh Atkins, John Whitehead, and many other correspondents for suggesting words, putting forward the *bêtes noires* in their semantic menageries, correcting mistakes, imperfections, ignorance, and misjudgment, and helping to rewrite the articles.

1/ BOOMERANGS

Old English favourites
are coming home to roost

Silly people grumble about English being corrupted by Americanisms. In fact the United States is the most creative and prolific source of vigour for the language, which lives because it keeps changing and growing. In any case, before grumbling about a new American vogue word, it is worth inspecting it carefully to see how new it really is. Many such words were exported across the Atlantic by our common ancestors. They have died or become archaic here; flourished over there; and are now coming home like boomerangs.

It is well known that the Elizabethans used 'fall' (a far more expressive word) to mean autumn, and 'gotten' as the past participle of to get. Fanny Burney, an accurate though irritating recorder of contemporary slang, has surprising examples of such boomerang words: *to meet up with, cute*, and *invite* as a noun meaning an invitation. *To make out*, meaning to succeed or thrive, was common in Ben Jonson's day, but became uncommon in British English in the nineteenth century. The *OED* marked it 'chiefly U.S.' Now it is coming back. Volume two of the *OED Supplement*, published in 1976, gives illustrations of its use in Britain again under American influence; for example, from the *Observer* in 1959: 'Whitsun seemed a good occasion to learn how Shakespeare and tourism were making out.'

I guess, in the sense I am pretty sure, was good English before it became good American. Some scholars think this use is evidenced in Chaucer, for example in *Parlement of Foules*, 'For thou of love hast lost thy tast, *I gesse*'. But this is disputed. The expression has come home to roost again as a general English use in Bringlish or BritEnglish.

Brash, meaning flash and rash, impudent and crude, seems to have been current in English dialects at the beginning of the nineteenth century, and then to have died out. It returned to Britain as a loanword from the United States in the 1920s.

1

The suffix -*wise*, as, rebarbatively, in *situationwise*, is not an odious American neologism but a respectable revenant from antiquity. Chaucer had *doublewise*; Bunyan, *dialoguewise*; and Coleridge, *maidenwise*.

Handy to, meaning near to, was common in English dialect in the nineteenth century, then died out. Volume two of the *OED Supplement, H-N*, gives illustrations to show how, under American influence, it has come home to the vocabulary of British English again. The same magnificent monument of scholarship shows how *hunch*, meaning a premonition or intuitive feeling that something will happen or may be the case, a presentiment, is not a recent American invention, but was originally launched from the respectable old English *hunch*, meaning a push, thrust, or shove. For example, from Muriel Spark in 1960: ' "Only a hunch", said Dougal. "I may be wrong." '

Other old boomerangs that are hurtling home across the Atlantic are: *to loan*, as a verb; *mad*, meaning angry; *car*, meaning railway carriage, which is the word used in notices about possible bombs in the London Underground; and perhaps *barber*, which is coming home to nest in our hair again, replacing the recent BritEnglish hairdresser. One of the great strengths of English is that it keeps open house, adopting the best new uses and old boomerangs from English-speakers all over the world.

The converse of a boomerang word is a word inherited from our common vocabulary of the eighteenth century that has survived in common usage in BritEnglish, but become obsolete in AmerEnglish. For example, the following sentence might be understood in the United States (it is risky to generalize about AmerEnglish, since usage varies widely throughout the continent), but it is not common usage: 'I am too mean to go to the seaside for a fortnight, so I reckon I will fetch my bathing costume and paddle in the bath.' The American translation of that is: 'I am too cheap to go to the ocean for two weeks, so I guess I will get my swimsuit and wade in the tub.'

'Fetch' is used in the United States mainly to describe dogs retrieving. Usage suggests that the custom of paddling, with the trousers rolled up to the knees and the braces (suspenders) shown proudly, is confined to the English seaside (ocean); and that Americans prefer to take the plunge right into wading, which sounds to English ears a wetter thing to do than paddling. The other principal words in the exemplary sentence all flourish in BritEnglish, but have gone

2

out of fashion and been replaced with new words across the ocean.

The Southern States appear to be more linguistically conservative than the Northern, perhaps because their English has been less affected by mass immigration of ethnic groups who are not native speakers of English. In the South they still talk of drawing a bath; elsewhere baths are run.

A third group of words are those that have survived in common usage in both BritEnglish and AmerEnglish, but have developed divergent meanings on either side of the Atlantic. *Homely* is the classic example of this group. It means 'cosy' in Britain, but 'plain' in the United States, and can accordingly be a cause of misunderstanding and offence. *To knock·up* is another Janus phrase with different meanings on either side of the Atlantic. In BritEnglish it means: 1. to wake someone up by banging on their door; 2. to warm up at tennis; 3. to throw together, as in knocking up a quick snack. In the United States *to knock up* is an indelicate phrase for getting a girl in a delicate condition. Its British use can be as startling to Americans as the American use of *fanny* is in Britain.

2/ CAMP

The high and low of camp

It is easier to recognize *camp* (adjective) as a cliquish shibboleth and password to fashionable intellectual circles than to define with precision what it means in a particular context. Kenneth Williams is a brilliant exponent of *camp* humour; but that is to give an example, not to define. The difficulty seems to be that two ideas are mixed together in the one word. The first connotation is homosexual; the second theatrical; and the two can be combined in any proportion.

The first and evidently the original meaning pertains to and is characteristic of homosexuals, especially when they are showing off with exaggerated effeminate mannerisms and gestures. The secondary and theatrical meaning has to do with something so outrageously artificial, affected, inappropriate, or banal that it is considered clever or amusing because of its unsophisticated artistic quality. As well as being an adjective, the word is used as a noun or a verb, with the optional and otiose string of prepositions favoured by current American usage tied on its tail, as in *camp* it up and *camp* around. As a verb it means to overact, to ham it up, to strut ostentatiously; you know, darling, to act in a deliciously *campy* manner: 'Most of the time he *camps* it up for sniggers with manly gestures fading into womanly wriggles.'

You can have *high camp*, as in almost all ballet and Baroque art; and *low camp*, which has been nicely defined as a female impersonator imitating Marlene Dietrich in a seedy nightclub. *Camp* is a gay sort of outdoor kitsch. So protean a word is not very useful, and is harmful to precision. It should be used only if the user knows exactly what he means by it, and could paraphrase his sentence without using it: a priggish recommendation that would cause the word *camp* in its new sense to vanish off the face of the earth. The bad and tiresome use is as an amusing fashionable password so woolly as to be worthless.

4

The Columbus of *camp* and its principal definer and popularizer was Susan Sontag in a seminal essay entitled 'Notes on *Camp*' in a 1964 issue of *Partisan Review*. She wrote: 'The essence of *camp* is its love of the unnatural: of artifice and exaggeration. And *camp* is esoteric—something of a private code, a badge of identity even, among small urban cliques.'

The origins and etymology of the word are obscure, but clearly queer. One ingenious theory, not recognized by the dictionaries, derives it from the acronym K.A.M.P., a label used in the New York City police files and standing for Known As Male Prostitute. From there it is supposed to have entered the slang of the 1930s as an adjective. As it gained wide circulation by word of mouth, most of its users were unaware of its origin. So, when they came to write it, they used the obvious spelling, *camp*.

Another even more fanciful and distinctly *camp* derivation suggests that the word came into use in England early in the nineteenth century, and continued for as long as it was the practice for soldiers to summer under canvas in Hyde Park. 'Going for a bit of *camp*' is alleged to have been the phrase used by the fops of the time who slipped under the awnings of the tents for assignations with the rapacious and licentious soldiery. No contemporary documentary evidence has yet been adduced to support this etymology.

The American Thesaurus of Slang (1942) lists as one meaning of *camp* 'a male homosexual brothel or gathering place'. Eric Partridge in *A Dictionary of the Underworld* (1950) suggested that the word came originally from the Antipodes. He listed examples of *camp* as an adjective being used in the 1930s as an Australian slang synonym for homosexual. And he cited earlier sources that gave *camp* as underworld slang for 'a low saloon' and 'a brothel'. The *OED Supplement* (volume one, 1972) discovered a use as early as 1909 in a book about English usage, which defined *camp* as: 'Actions and gestures of exaggerated emphasis. Probably from French. Used chiefly by persons of exceptional want of character. "How very *camp* he is." '

This sounds remarkably like the modern usage. But probably from the French? What can the fellow have had in mind? *'Je fiche le camp'*? Philip Hope-Wallace, the opera critic, a fastidious scholar, and a witness whose evidence must be taken seriously, claims persuasively to have read in provincial French music criticism the words: 'Monsieur Pont a su *camper* le rôle de Rigoletto

5

avec dignité.' He takes this to mean that M. Pont performed that role with nobility and vigour: 'Indeed to *camp* with dignity might be what Hamlet calls a consummation devoutly to be wished.'

3 / CHARISMA

*When everyone has charisma
then no one's charismatic*

Charisma is a technical term of theology that has recently been politicized by sociologists, and subsequently vulgarized into a vogue word by journalists and politicians. The change can be dated quite precisely for once. The new meaning became popular in the 1960s when John F. Kennedy was President. It well described the almost religious aura of leadership cultivated by the White House, and the corresponding quasi-religious enthusiasm of J.F.K.'s disciples.

The word was originally New Testament Greek, pronounced with an initial 'k' sound, and generally used in the plural as *charismata*. It means the gifts of God's grace: the blessings, spiritual and temporal, bestowed on every Christian for the due fulfilment of his vocation. In a narrower sense the word is used for the supernatural graces that individual Christians need to promote the spiritual advancement of their fellows. In 1 Corinthians 12 these spiritual gifts or *charismata* are enumerated as: the word of wisdom, the word of knowledge, faith, the gifts of healing, the working of miracles, prophecy, discerning of spirits, the gift of tongues, and the interpretation of tongues.

The Early Church was troubled by *Charismatics,* holy men and ascetics, who travelled around prophesying, speaking with tongues, and otherwise making a spectacle of themselves, and lived by begging. In his *Second Epistle to the Thessalonians* St Paul wrote against these wild *charismatic* drop-outs: 'For we hear that there are some which walk among you disorderly, working not at all, and are busybodies.' He instructed his followers in Thessalonia to ensure that 'if a man does not work, neither shall he eat'.

In Constantinople in the Middle Ages *charisma* was used to refer to the condition of berserk frenzy induced by drugs, religious mania, or convulsive fits. *Charismatics* were used as military auxiliaries to encourage the Christian troops and put the fear of God into the enemy.

For centuries *charisma* kept itself to itself in its neat, narrow cope of theological meaning, and was not found outside specialist religious writings. Then around the end of the nineteenth century and the beginning of the twentieth the word began to be used tentatively as a metaphor. Rudolph Sohm, the jurist and historian of the Protestant church, used *charisma* as a fairly strict metaphor for certain secular ascriptions.

The word had its connotations widely secularized by Max Weber in his *Wirtschaft und Gesellschaft* published in German in 1922 after his death. This work was first translated into English in 1947 by A. M. Henderson and Talcott Parsons with the title *Max Weber's Theory of Social and Economic Organization*. In his book Weber defined his new use: 'The term *charisma* will be applied to a certain quality of an individual personality by virtue of which he is set apart from ordinary men and treated as endowed with supernatural, superhuman, or at least specifically exceptional powers or qualities.' Weber's use was widely adopted into international sociologese from 1922 onwards. In a correspondence arising out of the first publication of this article Robert Burchfield, chief editor of the Oxford English dictionaries, traced earlier English uses of *charismatic* (1929) and *charisma* (1930) in Weber's sense than are recorded in the *OED Supplement*.

Sociologists are notoriously cavalier and innovationist with language, as people who chose for their discipline a name that is a monstrous miscegenation of Latin with Greek might be expected to be. Sociology as a name was invented by the French philosopher, Auguste Comte (1798-1857). Comte appears to have had some misgivings about the word's hybrid character, but he considered that there was some 'compensation for this etymological defect, in the fact that it recalls the two historical sources—the one intellectual, the other social—from which modern civilization has sprung'.

Sociologists are in any case more tempted by gobbledygook than other academics, because their subject is everyday life, which ordinary people also think that they know about, and presume to talk about. Nuclear physicists and ancient historians have subjects and vocabularies beyond the ken of ordinary mortals. Sociologists deal with such commonplace though important matters as homes and families, work and play. Therefore they tend to invent high-flown jargon to demonstrate that when they talk about commonplace matters they are doing so in a scientific and superior way, and not as other men do. So the English language is abused and polluted. It

8

is a pity that they and the psychologists (also grave offenders against the language) do not employ a team of philosophers and philologists as specialists in words and meanings to construct their jargon for them.

After the sociologists had sunk their claws into *charisma*, the fashionable mob followed. There is an apt early example of Andreas Papandreou selecting the Greek word in an interview in 1966: 'I do not need George Papandreou (his father). I am the only other man in the party with such *charisma*.' It is now widely applied to celebrated personalities, especially political candidates, and can be roughly equated with strong personal appeal, glamour, magnetism, or, changing from a theological to a physiological metaphor, political sex appeal.

Kennedy notoriously had *charisma*; Nixon and Ford have not; Jimmy Carter just may have some. Khrushchev had it; Brezhnev and Kosygin have not; and Stalin certainly did not have it. Pope John had it; Pope Paul has not. General de Gaulle had it; Giscard d'Estaing does not quite have it, though he may attain it if he becomes a grand old man. No British politician for years has had *charisma*, though both Harold Macmillan 'Supermac' and Sir Harold Wilson tried unsuccessfully to attract some of the *charisma* from the nimbus of J.F.K. Curiously, because of the sentimental British attitude to old age, the older British politicians grow and the longer they have been out of office, the more signs of incipient *charisma* they show. People forget what they were like when they had power. *Charisma* in a public figure is something more than style, but something less than vision. It can be a specious quality, implying little more than that its possessor has the combination of superficial charm, attractiveness, political sex appeal, and sincerity that makes a good candidate for office.

There seems to be no good reason for preferring *charisma* if some such equivalent will do the job. And it would be thrifty to reserve the word for religious contexts, where it may be useful to speak of a *charismatic* leader, who embodies the charm of the movement in his person. If it must be used in other contexts, the person to whom it is applied should be worthy of such a grand word. It is just possible to apply it to a world statesman, if you must. To apply it wantonly to a pop singer or a television personality, where it means no more than charm, is further to debase a word that has already been sadly debased.

Perhaps journalists are surfeited with over-indulgence in the

9

word; perhaps modern politicians of all countries are so conspicuously unattractive that it would be absurd to attribute *charisma* to them; perhaps we live in a disillusioned age that makes us reluctant to attribute supernatural or superhuman qualities to any of our contemporaries. Whatever the reason, the tide may have turned, and *charisma* seems to be returning to its proper homes in theology and sociology: that is, to the world of learning.

4/ CHAUVINISM

Male chauvinist pigs are bores

Chauvinism and *chauvinist* (as in male *chauvinist* pig, *passim* in liberated discourse) are vogue words that have been widely popularized by the Women's Liberation Movement in the United States. As a consequence, they tend to be used in inappropriate contexts, and with more emotion than precision. In the war between the sexes *chauvinism* was a brilliantly successful slogan to describe an attitude of superiority towards members of the opposite sex (usually in our society male superiority), or behaviour exemplifying such a patronizing attitude, as in 'it is a sexist fallacy to fight male *chauvinism* with female *chauvinism*'. (Sexist is another successfully expressive technical term of Women's Lib that has come into the common language.) Because *chauvinism* is so successful and so powerful a word, its use has been extended, diluting its particular meaning and spilling over into the proper territory of such words as nationalism and patriotism.

The primary meaning of *chauvinism* is exaggerated patriotism of a bellicose sort, for which the French originally coined the phrase *'idolatrie napoléonienne'*. *Chauvinism* was a name invented for a nineteenth-century French quality, for which the closest contemporary British equivalent was 'Jingoism'.

The eponym of *chauvinism* was Nicolas *Chauvin*, a French fusilier born at Rochefort, whose simple-minded heroism and devotion to Napoleon made his name a byword, and eventually an eponymous word in its own right. His military career, in parts at any rate, appears to have been legendary in the old-fashioned and precise sense of the adjective. He is said to have been wounded seventeen times during the French Revolutionary and Napoleonic wars, naturally always in the front, never turning his back to the enemy. He had three fingers chopped off, a shoulder fractured, and his forehead horribly mutilated: and was rewarded for his services with a sword of honour, a red ribbon, and a pension of two hundred

11

francs. The battered old soldier came to typify the cult of military glory and sacrificial patriotism that was popular after Waterloo among the embittered veterans of Napoleon's armies.

Eventually, when aggressive militarism went out of fashion, *Chauvin* came to be a figure of fun, because of his simple-minded devotion to Napoleon and his extravagant belief in glory and the superiority of everything French. Satire, lampoons, and caricature during the 1830s ridiculed *Chauvin* as the exemplar of naïve and blind patriotism, and *chauvinisme* in French came to mean ultra-nationalism of any kind, whether Bonapartist or not. A popular play of 1831 called *La Cocarde Tricolore* by Charles T. and Jean Hippolyte Cogniard made *Chauvin* a ridiculous household name, and secured his name its place in the dictionaries. In it a silly old soldier called *Chauvin* sang a highly satirical song, *La Chanson du Chameau,* which made all France laugh and hum the tune. In the Third Republic, when there were conflicts between the civil and military authorities, the civilians called the militarist groups hostile to the Republic *chauvinists,* on the ground that they wanted to turn the whole state into a barracks.

Chauvin marched farther than France. His fame spread to Italy, where he gave his name to the braggadocian quality of *sciovinismo.* And he crossed the Channel into English in the middle of the nineteenth century. Significantly, one of the examples in the *Oxford English Dictionary* declares: 'Educated men are supposed to see the difference between patriotism and *Chauvinism.*' The recent modish development of Nicolas *Chauvin*'s legacy to the language has weakened that difference.

If it remains true to its engagingly ludicrous founding father, the word *chauvinism* ought to mean an exaggerated and naïve nationalism that looks down its nose on lesser breeds without the Law. It was an appropriate and effective derogatory metaphor to apply to males who regard females as naturally their inferiors, because of the supposed virtue of the masculine sex. The trouble is that it has become such a popular cliché that it is used automatically and indiscriminately instead of nationalism and patriotism, which are natural and can be positive words. *Chauvin* was a dangerous fool. But he did not make all nationalism and all patriotism dangerous and foolish.

5/ CLINICAL

How clinical is your bedside manner?

It is time that we had a *clinical* examination of *clinical*, which shows symptoms of becoming bedridden and transformed by a degenerative wasting disease. The word is directly derived from the Greek word for bed, though members of the oldest profession concerned with beds, or indeed with anything else, do not use it. Members of the medical profession, however, use *clinical* to mean : of or pertaining to the sick-bed, specifically to the sick-bed of indoor hospital patients. It refers not so much to the person in the hospital bed as to the person beside the bed, and even he prides himself on his bedside rather than his *clinical* manner. Accordingly medical men, whose word it was, have *clinical* tuition, *clinical* research, *clinical* problems, *clinical* deans (in some medical schools), and *clinical* specialities, all referring to the care of patients, primarily in bed. Even members of the veterinary profession use the word, though few of their patients are treated in beds.

The contrasting adjective is, in many cases, *laboratory*. Some laboratory workers even use *clinical* pejoratively, to mean unscientific, cosy, and bedside-mannered : smoothing the fevered brow on the lace-edged pillow. Other branches of the medical profession can be more exact in their work. The bacteriologists and other laboratory workers can grow a culture and examine it before committing themselves. The pathologists can open up the remains of their patients to look inside and see what went wrong; and so can the surgeons, though their view is more limited. But the *clinician* has to work by guess and by God, and accordingly tends to be regarded by his *preclinical* and *paraclinical* colleagues as woolly, vague, and inexact.

Journalists, advertising copywriters, and other magpies of technical terms have seized this sharp, precise word, and, as usual, got hold of the wrong end of the thermometer. They use it to mean something like coldly detached and dispassionate, bare and functional, as under laboratory conditions; in effect, the precise opposite of the original, medical, bedside-mannered usage. So we have bathrooms and new pieces of kitchen equipment described *passim* in the glossy ads and the puff-prose that goes with them as *clinical*; and even, if they are unlucky, as *sophisticated* as well.

What the writer evidently has in mind is that they have clean lines, steel taps, white plastic surfaces, and the functional design of laboratory equipment. What purist medical men infer from this new meaning is that the equipment is covered with a pink-tasselled counterpane, and has a bowl of chrysanthemums and a bunch of withered grapes sitting on it. Sensitive *clinical* doctors are upset that laymen understand their epithet to mean dispassionate, cold-blooded, and even computer-like, which is not the impression that their bedside manner seeks to give. The bedside doctor is and always must be involved with his patient.

When the cricket correspondent of *The Times* described an innings by Geoff Boycott as 'ruthless, *clinical*, dedicated, and timely', he evidently meant that Boycott was batting in a coldly detached and dispassionate manner, not in a soothing and sympathetic one.

In medical jargon the word has sired some entertaining offspring, including *preclinical* and *subclinical*. It may be true, as suggested by the popularized portrayals of hospital life by cinema and television, that *preclinical* medical students are always ready to jump into bed. But it is unlikely that in later years they will ever have to dive under beds in pursuit of patients with elusive *subclinical* conditions. Medical men use *subclinical* to describe an illness detectable by laboratory tests, but not yet apparent to the patient (or the *clinical* doctor) through symptoms and signs.

Clinical is an instructive example of a modern popularized technicality. Trade statistics are studied *clinically*; crimes are solved *clinically*; football sides are even said to be destroyed *clinically*; which sounds as if somebody is breaking his Hippocratic oath. But it will do the doctors little good to cry 'foul' about the vulgar misapprehension and expect some linguistic referee to blow his whistle. *Clinical* is well on the way to joining the melancholy catalogue of words whose meanings have been corrupted by greedy magpies of shiny technical vocabulary.

Thus, students of the Attic theatre complain in vain that it is impossible to have more than one protagonist in any given situation: the chief actor who took the principal part in a play by Aeschylus,

Sophocles, Euripides, or their peers. The ignorant, deceived by the word's accidental resemblance to antagonist, carry on regardless, using it in the plural as if it meant something like champions, or advocates, or defenders. They speak of a chief protagonist, or the protagonist of a cause or a person. Perhaps we could do something to resuscitate the real protagonist by reviving the use of his colleague, the deuteragonist, to describe the person who plays the part of second importance in a real or metaphorical drama.

Similarly architects complain in vain that flamboyant has a precise technical meaning: the French style contemporary with English Perpendicular, characterised by tracery whose wavy lines suggest the shape or motion of tongues of flame. Ignorant magpies carry on regardless, using it to mean florid, or flashy, or, well, you know what I mean, flamboyant.

So *clinical* is inexorably coming to mean something like its opposite; and the doctors will have to put up with it, or invent a new word for their specialized purpose. There is poetic justice of a sort if this happens. Members of the medical profession have often been unscrupulous and piratical Jargonauts with other men's jargon themselves.

6/ CLOUD-CUCKOO-LAND

Getting lost among the clouds

'If the previous speaker seriously believes that, he is living in *Cloud-Cuckoo-Land*' : *passim* in modern political discourse. Where on earth is this popular and by now heavily over-populated kingdom?

Cloud-Cuckoo-Land is in the process of becoming a derogatory vogue word, supposed to mean a silly sort of place, part away with the birds, part cuckoo, part castle-in-the-air, and wholly undesirable. Before this process is complete, it is worth recalling that *Cloud-Cuckoo-Land* was originally a very desirable and highly successful state. The modern historical error is not so gross as the other prevalent misapprehension that King Canute imagined that he could stop the tide coming in. But it is instructive of the way that the ceaseless tide of language erodes the meaning of words, and sometimes stands usage or history on its head.

(It was, of course, not Canute the Great who asserted that he was such a very important person that even the tide would obey his command, but his sycophantic courtiers. Canute got his feet wet on purpose, as a dramatic rebuke of their flattery. The story is recorded by Henry the Archdeacon of Huntingdon (1084?-1155) in his *Historia Anglorum*. He adds that as a gesture of humility Canute would never thereafter wear his crown, but hung it on the head of an effigy of the crucified Christ. The story may well be pious ecclesiastical legend with an improving moral. But it is a curious paradox that in careless rhetoric Canute has now become an exemplar of an infatuated and arrogant reactionary who seriously believes that he can turn back the tides, usually those unpersuasively historicist currents, the tides of history.)

To return from that watery digression to confusion in the clouds : *The Birds*, by Aristophanes, was first performed at the Great Dionysia of 414 BC. Its plot concerns an ingenious Athenian called Peisthetairos, 'Persuader', who persuades the birds to build them-
16

selves a city in the clouds, and so compels the besieged gods to accept humiliating terms.

Like all comedies by Aristophanes, it combines witty and fantastic farce with distinctly sharp satire and schoolboy scurrility about prominent Athenians. Even the slowest member of the audience could grasp the satirical connexion between the visionary ambitions of the birds and the imperialist ambitions of Athens, which had just launched against Sicily the most formidable armament that had ever issued from a Greek harbour. Perhaps Aristophanes's master-piece took only second prize because it outraged Athenian jingoism, or even Athenian chauvinism.

Nephelococcygia, *Cloud-Cuckoo-Land,* was indeed fantastic, but in the play it was crowned with brilliant success. It is shown to be in many ways a better place than either Athens or Heaven. For ex-ample, common informers, sophists, and other plagues of contem-poraneous Athens are refused entry; Miss World herself comes down to marry Peisthetairos, bringing with her, in addition to Zeus's capitulation, good counsels, happy laws, sound common sense, and all the other blessings that were fast disappearing from fifth-century Greece, to say nothing of vegetarianism, at least as far as concerns the flesh of birds.

The abuse of *Cloud-Cuckoo-Land* as a vague derogatory meta-phor, with an imposing ring of spurious learning, is comparatively recent. Victorian politicians, who knew their classics, never used it so. The first Victorian translations rendered the place, less eupho-niously, as Cuckoo-Cloud-Land and Cloudcuckoobury.

In 1899 the first use of *Cloud-Cuckoo-Land* as a depreciatory metaphor was recorded : 'All his thinking processes fade off into the logic of *Cloud-Cuckoo-Land.*' On the contrary, *Cloud-Cuckoo-Land* was conceived originally as being in many ways more logical than the real world, and in every way more logical than the heavenly world. Evidently the cuckoo component of the name accentuates for English speakers the craziness of the Never-Never, happy, far-off, paradisal, and infinitely desirable *Cloud-Cuckoo-Land.* So it has now become an overused vogue word for a silly and unpleasant fantasy. Robert Graves poetically captured exactly the unfashion-ably desirable and beautiful nature of the place, when he wrote :

'Kingfishers, when they die,
To far Cloud-Cuckoo pastures fly.'

Utopia, Sir Thomas More's imaginary island, has not been so much worsened as *Cloud-Cuckoo-Land.* Sir Thomas in *Utopia,* his principal literary work, first published in 1516, describes 'Nowhere land', which enjoys a perfect social, legal, and political system. Communism is the general law; a national system of education is extended to men and women alike; and there is complete freedom of religion. It was all very unlike life under the Tudors. From this influential book *Utopian* has come in modern rhetoric to mean impracticably ideal and visionary; but not actually undesirable like *Cloud-Cuckoo-Land*. *Erewhon* (an anagram of *nowhere*), Samuel Butler's satirical romance about an imaginary land, has not been widely adopted and misinterpreted as a popular metaphor, perhaps because of the outlandish appearance of the name, and the difficulty of pronouncing it. It seems a sad fact of language that imaginary ideal societies rapidly lose their ideals when they are bandied about in the rude world of practical politics.

7/ TO COMPOUND

A compounded nuisance

A funny thing has happened to the verb *to compound* on its way from the law courts. Over the past few years, too recently to be recorded in the latest dictionaries, it has acquired a new meaning, startlingly different from its old meanings, and in some contexts their opposite. The new meaning is therefore confusing. It also threatens to oust the old meanings from their nest. It would simplify and purify the language if we could find some way of *compounding* the confusion.

To compound always used to mean: (1) to compact together, combine, or compose; to mix; (2) to compromise, settle a debt by agreement, or commute a periodical payment with a lump sum; (3) to forbear to prosecute for a consideration, hence the offence of *compounding* a felony. These modest but useful meanings are the ones that might reasonably be expected from a word directly derived from the Latin *componere,* itself a translation of the Greek word from which *synthesis* is derived. Composition is the noun of *to compound.*

What seems to have caused the confusion is that non-lawyers have misapprehended the meaning of *to compound* a felony. This is the offence of agreeing not to prosecute somebody in return for some consideration, usually, as the world runs, financial. Outsiders hazily mistook the phrase to mean to aggravate the seriousness of a felony. And, before you could say Fowler, the erroneous meaning had become a raging popularized technicality. It is now widely abused to mean: to make worse, aggravate, multiply, increase, and even, in a vogue word that is equally unpleasant but at any rate not ambiguous, to escalate. The printed and spoken word is widely contaminated by such uses as: the high unemployment figures are *compounded* by the failure of the Government to do something. Injustices are regularly and mysteriously *compounded* by somebody's negative attitude; and difficulties are *compounded* by

19

somebody else's failure to recognize something or other The educated reader at first naturally takes such a use of the verb to mean to condone or to fail to take action against. That way confusion lies.

It is probable that this new meaning has evolved not from the law courts, but from the banks and other counting-houses. Bankers, actuaries, and schoolchildren in mathematics classes understand that at 'Five per cent *compound*' a sum of money doubles itself in fourteen, not twenty years. *Compound* interest, which accumulates at an accelerating rate, may be the source of the verb *to compound*'s coming to mean to increase or multiply. In a flexible and adaptive language such as English words are always apt to gain by association. A *compound,* meaning the enclosed land around a house or factory, probably comes from the Malayan word *kampong,* meaning an enclosure.

There is nothing against words getting themselves new meanings: and even if there is, there is precious little that anybody can do to stop the process. But if a word already has a perfectly good meaning, and if its new meaning is already perfectly adequately expressed by old words, the change muddies the language and makes it less precise. The new use of *to compound* is just such a nuisance, and should be resisted by all who care for the language.

In particular, to use *to compound* in its accountant's sense in a context that sounds suitable for the law courts is to invite misunderstanding. For example, to write 'he *compounded* the offence' (when what is meant is that he did something to aggravate the offence) is to vex every lawyer who reads the sentence, and to provoke numbers of them to litigious correspondence in defence of their jargon.

8/ CONSENSUS

The overworked word
at the centre of politics

For the past decade *consensus* has regularly been in the top ten of fashionable vogue words. The *OED* judged that the word was not naturalized; but it noted two specialized uses. The first was physiological: a general concord of different parts or organs of the body, as in (from a psychological work): a mutually dependent set of organs having a *consensus* of functions. The second was scholarly, particularly in classical scholarship, as was fitting for a word that wears its Latinity so conspicuously on its sleeve. In this use *consensus* means agreement in opinion, and is particularly used to describe the collective unanimous opinion of a number of persons or sources. Example: the *consensus* of manuscripts X, Y, and Z leaves no room for doubt about a reading. Since *consensus* itself means agreement in opinion, the common error of talking about the *consensus* of opinion is, to take a charitable view, tautological; to take an uncharitable view, rubbish.

The word also has a long history as a term of ecclesiastical jargon to describe the common mind of church authorities. Thus, at the Council of Trent (1543-63) Pope Pius IV emphasized that 'he wished to define only that which had been decided by the unanimous *consensus* of the Church Fathers'. Modern ecumenical writing uses the word to express something more than the theological middle ground. For example, the International Commission of Anglicans and Roman Catholics, in its 'Agreed Statements' on Eucharistic doctrine and the ministry, declared that its members were convinced that they 'had reached agreement on essential points of doctrine', that 'nothing essential had been omitted', and that *consensus* had therefore been attained. In other words *consensus* in the field of Christian doctrine need not involve compromise of principle.

From the 1960s the word found a useful new meaning to describe the broad middle ground of politics, where the great, sensible majority of men of good will are supposed to agree on policies that are distasteful only to extremist minorities and fringe fanatics in their private Caves of Adullam. The modern vogue epithets for such outsiders from the *consensus* are Marxists, 'Trots' (Trotskyites), fascists, and other such words that have lost most of their descriptive content and become mere abuse. *Consensus* arrived in the vocabulary just too late to describe the middle ground between the Labour right and the Conservative left in the 1950s. So we invented Butskellism, a hybrid by Rab Butler out of Hugh Gaitskell, instead.

Consensus came to be widely used to describe not some particular set of policy ideas, but rather a presumed substratum of unanimously agreed principles that underlies our (or indeed any stable) system of government. Quinquennial elections, the principle of the National Health Service, and much of the rest of the Welfare State are now part of the *consensus* of British politics, because no serious and substantial politician wants to do away with them, though some certainly want to modify them. In practice such woolly principles have been found to be diffuse and of little practical consequence; and the recent tendency towards extremism and despair in British politics has concentrated politicians at their opposing poles, and depopulated the moderate middle ground of *consensus*.

A more cynical way of describing *consensus* is to see it as the agreement by which the major parties agree to co-operate in order to keep the political initiative and power in parliamentary hands. Here is an engaging early example from *Peace News* in 1968: 'Cicero is a more dubious case: an unsuccessful *consensus* politician, if ever I saw one.' That may be poor Roman history; but it is a good example of the new use to describe the politics of the centre. Cicero himself wrote that 'the *consensus* among all nations on whatever matter may be taken for the law of nature': which is farther than most people would care to go with the English word.

Consensus does a useful job that nothing else quite does to describe the middle ground of politics. Like all useful new words it is now so grossly overused that every recurrence of it grates on the fastidious. It should be reserved for its specific political and social context, and for the learned *consensus* of evidence, texts, organs, or bishops. To use it simply as an impressive synonym for agreement exposes the user to the charge of pomposity and Gadarene trendiness. The illiteracy of misspelling the word CONCENSUS, as if it

22

were derived from some fraudulent public opinion poll, is prevalent, either through ignorance or misprint. If it has been so misspelled in this chapter, let us hope that it was misprinted.

9/ COSMETIC

Putting on a new face

We live in a *cosmetic* age, as the powder-puff said to the lip-stick. *Cosmetics* and fashion have become big business, and, therefore, are taken seriously. We value image and public relations more than the solid flesh behind the paint. So it is not surprising that the jargon of fashion is being adopted figuratively.

Over the past few years *cosmetic* itself has come to be widely used as a metaphor, as both noun and adjective. The word comes originally from the Greek verb meaning to adorn or embellish. It is a short step from its primary meaning of an artificial aid for improving the appearance, to something that covers up the blemishes, and improves the appearance of things other than faces. The Nixon administration was notorious for using such words as 'inoperative' as *cosmetics* to delude the public and perhaps even itself.

From there *cosmetic* as an adjective has come to be used as meaning both decorative (for embellishment) and deceitful. A drunken politician gets himself photographed drinking tea at a local temperance fête for *cosmetic* purposes. And from there it is another short step to the meaning superficial, insincere, or lacking in depth or thoroughness. An unpopular and timid government introduces *cosmetic* measures just before an election in the hope, generally justified, that a week is a long time in politics, and that the memory of the public is as short as its belief in politicians' promises is bottomless. Webster's *6000 Words,* 1976 (the words in the title being those that have come into the common language since *Webster's Third New International Dictionary* was published in 1971) exemplifies the new use with a quotation about some anonymous property developer who 'bought up older homes in declining neighborhoods, fixed them up with *cosmetic* repairs, and sold them at inflated values'.

Hence has come the verb *to cosmeticize,* meaning to make more attractive or easier to accept. In its literal sense of to treat with

24

cosmetics the verb is more than a century old; for example, from 1860: 'The skins that were not hard red, were of a ghastly *cosmeticized* whiteness.' It is now used to mean to make (usually something unpleasant, ugly, or unpopular) superficially attractive. *Playboy* commended a book for seeing a singer whole with the immortal words: 'This is not a flack's *cosmeticized* biography.' (A flack is an expressively contemptuous word of unknown derivation for a press agent.)

Another new metaphor from fashion is the verb *to highlight*. As a noun *highlight* is at least three hundred years old, and means the brightest part of an object or representation of it in painting, and thence in photography and cinematography. The word has been adopted by the *cosmetics* industry, particularly hairdressing. From Vidal Sassoon a verb, both transitive and intransitive, has been derived by way of the photographic jargon for illuminating a print with vivid distinctness.

It can mean: either (transitively) to centre attention upon, to cause to loom large in importance or urgency; or (intransitively) to constitute a *highlight* or distinctive feature of. Particularly in the transitive sense it is a raging vogue word in broadcasting. It is difficult to listen to a news bulletin without having several things *highlighted* (or should it be *lit*?). Older words such as emphasize, stress, and underline are quite unemployed.

There is nothing objectionable in these new metaphors in moderation. In some contexts they are vivid and apt. New metaphors are a constant source of reinvigoration for the language. But at present these *cosmetic* metaphors are laid on so thick and are so overworked by the fashionable that they are in danger of becoming fashionable non-words: good for one season, and then tedious and a laughing-stock, as tasteless as a woman whose painted lips spread all over her face.

10/ ETHNIC

We are all ethnics under the skin

One of the most famous fashion houses in the Mayfair rag trade regularly advertises its new lines, in language of fashionable vacuity, as 'Touch of *Ethnic*'. Just to make sure that the message sinks in, the advertisement parrots fatuously on: 'One of the prettiest versions of the *ethnic* look around. Super contrasting *ethnic* pattern on sleeves.' What does it think it means by this new use of the adjective? The garment illustrated and modelled by what appears to be a member of the Anglo-Saxon race is a tunic top with striped and patterned sleeves.

In the past few years *ethnic* has become popular, primarily in the United States, as both adjective and noun to describe a member of an *ethnic* group, especially one who retains the customs, language, or social views of his group. *Ethnic* has come to mean foreign, exotic, or un-American; a polite term for Jews, Poles, Italians, and other supposedly lesser breeds just inside the Law.

Sometimes it is used to make a distinction between *ethnics,* who are immigrants or descendants of immigrants with whitish faces, who cling to their common racial, cultural, religious, or linguistic characteristics within the wider host community, and 'coloureds', who form similar minority groups, but have darkish faces. The *OED Supplement* found an example as early as 1945, not surprisingly in a work of sociology, that hot spring of potent new jargon: 'The Irish had their origins largely in the peasant stratum. The Jews were of the burgher class. These differences in the *ethnics'* social-class background will be seen later to have important bearing on their adaptation.'

It is a silly word for the purpose since we are all of us, Wasp or Gentile, members of some race and nation, even if we renounce it, - or consider it to be so superior to all other races that it is not really a race at all, but an apotheosis that all men envy, or ought to envy.

The word has an interesting and not inappropriate history, having always been used to make patronizing racial and class distinctions. It comes from the Greek word for a race or nation. *Ethnic* came to be used in the Koine, the common literary Greek of the New Testament, to mean heathen or Gentile. This scriptural meaning was so dominant that early English philologists derived the word from 'heathenic' by a process of bogus popular etymology. In English from 1470 onwards the adjective *ethnic* was used to mean pertaining to nations not Christian or Jewish; Gentile, heathen, pagan. The secondary meaning of pertaining to race, peculiar to a race or nation, ethnological, is not recorded until 1851. A dark early example of this secondary use is: 'Heresies are at best *ethnic*; truth is essentially catholic.'

There are those who raise an eyebrow at the modern American use of *ethnic* as a substantive. It is therefore interesting and amusing that *ethnic* as noun is recorded earlier in English than *ethnic* as adjective. A work of hagiography of 1375 has: 'A part of the temple fell down and made a great destruction of *ethnics*.' The old noun in its primary meaning, like the old adjective, means somebody from the wrong sort of race, neither Christian nor Jew: a Gentile, heathen, or pagan, who deserves to have his idolatrous temple fall on him.

It is an agreeable merry-go-round of language that this exclusive racial and religious epithet of the New Testament has come back into use as a euphemistic term for racial and religious minorities. '*Ethnic* Christmas cards with black, brown, or yellow Santas testify to the fact that the American melting pot is still bubbling, despite gloomy assertions to the contrary.' There it is a polite and positive way of saying 'racialist', or, in its entirely otiose new variant, 'racist'. Words describing race are notoriously volatile and sensitive for modern users of language. The *OED Supplement* has revised its editorial policy in the 1970s to hang out warning signals in front of many such *ethnic* words to indicate that they are offensive and abusive. It may not be a satisfactory word, but *ethnic* as noun and adjective at present does a job that is not done as well by any other word. And, as the advertisements in the fashionable frock shops show, it is establishing itself rather hazily in British English also.

11 / EUPHORIA

*Let us adopt a sophisticated stance
of conservative euphoria*

The growth of a living language is a history of a continuous process of change, authoritatively exemplified in the *OED*, which is a dictionary of the history of words; that is, a record of their changes. Words acquire new meanings and yield up old meanings under the ceaseless erosion of the tides of communication. The changes in meanings tend to be utilitarian and for the general good. If they are not, like other fads they usually fade away.

Here follow some words that are actively in the process of changing their meanings. Of most of them it is too early to judge whether the change is fixed, or merely a transient fashion, soon to be forgotten by all except the patient Oxford lexicographer:

Euphoria (ic): by its Greek derivation and long usage it was once a learned word, alternatively spelled *euphory*, meaning a state of cheerfulness or well-being, of feeling good. Note Auden's delicious:

'Come peregrine nymph, display your warm
Euphoric flanks in their full glory.'

The word is a vogue craze, coming to mean optimism, over-confidence, or even, analogously with the common misuse of optimism, merely hoping.

In delightful botanical nomenclature *Euphoria* is the name of a genus of the family *Sapindaceae*, and consists of six species of trees that are natives of Southern Asia. They are allied to *Litchi*, but have petals and a deeply lobed five-partite imbricate calyx. Sir Joseph Paxton, the famous botanist and ornamental gardener of the early nineteenth century, explained the Greek origin of the name as meaning that the *Euphoric* trees carry their fruit well and are fertile. The fruit is globose or elliptic, about an inch across. All of this it is possible potently and powerfully to believe without agreeing that 'he is *euphoric* about his chances' is a good way of saying that he is hopeful about his chances.

Sophisticated: until recently was pejorative, meaning adulterated;
28

not pure; altered from primitive simplicity; falsified; not honest; and so on. Its new meaning is commendatory and applied either to persons, ideas, or machinery: up-to-date, complex, modishly clever. There is an interesting and depressing parable about our society embedded in the change.

Backlog: started life literally as a *back log,* a large log put at the back of a fire to support the rest and keep it going through the night, especially in the heartier parts of the colonies, where men were men and camp fires were camp fires. The earliest use recorded by the *OED* comes from the North American colonies in 1684: 'The spit came down with the point foremost, and stuck in the *back-log.*' By extension and metaphor *backlog* came to mean a reserve built up deliberately. Now it is coming to mean arrears of unfulfilled orders resulting from a strike, or passengers delayed at an airport by a fog, or other incongruous extended applications, with no hint of deliberation or of the *backlog* having been put there on purpose: the very opposite. The metaphor is still warm, and twitches under the abuse.

Alternative etymologies have been suggested for *backlog,* though they are not supported by the dictionaries. A lumberman wrote from Canada to say that by *backlog* he understood that there were a lot of logs backing up the river, and therefore difficult to move, and sometimes wasted: in other words a log-jam. An ancient mariner asserted that *backlog* was a nautical term meaning arrears of the ship's log-book, which had to be made up when there was time to spare from navigation and other more pressing nautical business. These rival derivations are ingenious, and either would be a better justification for the metaphorical extension of the word. However, they are not persuasive. The camp fire etymology is old, well-established, and widespread from Canada and the United States to Australia and New Zealand.

Fulsome: used to be a regular Uriah Heep of a word, with strong intimations of over-demonstrative insincerity and fawning. It seems to be losing its slimy connotations. A recent Reuter's dispatch from Moscow referred to the *fulsome* praise of Mr Brezhnev by delegates to the Communist Party Congress. Sadly no rudeness was intended by cautious Reuter's. The context makes it clear that all that was meant was that the tributes were the most extensive, heavy, and noteworthy since Khrushchev celebrated his seventieth birthday.

Conservative: in one sense used to mean characterized by caution or moderation. Hence it has come by way of the United States to mean purposely or deliberately low in reference to estimates, as in: 'The distances quoted are *conservative*.' Here is another American example: 'It is *conservative* to say that between two and three months were spent in the drafting of a document which in the end was rejected by the Senate.' Not just estimates, but investments, bankers, architectural styles, and even suits are described as *conservative*. This still sounds slightly odd in the United Kingdom, perhaps because one of the principal political parties has adopted *Conservative* as its name.

Stance: originally meant standing-place, station, or position, as with legs crossed, head in air, and curses on the lips in that hell-hole bunker on the thirteenth. It has now been widely adopted by the fashionable to signify attitude, view, or opinion. This often causes the unwary user to put his foot in it and adopt an absurd *stance*, since the metaphor is new and the original meaning, firmly grounded on the feet, is not yet stone dead.

Not all these changes are fixed; not all are for the bad. But the motive for most of the changes seems to be the bad but common one of preferring a long, woolly, impressive word to a more precise everyday one.

12/ FRUITION

*Deciding whether an inchoate word
gets the fruition of a work permit*

English is a hospitable language, as England is traditionally a hospitable country. One of the glories of the English language is that it welcomes in and naturalizes its vocabulary from every other tongue. It combines and adopts useful words from Anglo-Saxon and Teutonic roots alongside Latin, French, Greek, Hindi, Australian, AmerEnglish, and anything else that comes to tongue, with majestic disinterestedness. It is foolish to take a strict Powellite attitude to such verbal immigration, for instance by appointing a board of linguistic immigration officers, such as they have across the Channel, to preserve the racial purity of the native tongue. English is a superb tool for communication just because it is flexible, unregulated, demotic, and unracialist. Our mongrelism is a source of linguistic as well as of national strength.

At the same time we should not have a policy of entirely unrestricted linguistic immigration. An alien word should have a work permit to prove that it is going to do a job not already being done by a native, before it is allowed to settle. Otherwise it is pretentious neophilia to prefer a fancy foreign word to an old-established native. To say *ambience* or *ambiance* (the French spelling) if you mean nothing more than atmosphere, surroundings, or environment is vulgar showing-off.

But to resist all change in the form either of new words from abroad or of new jobs for old words is reaction, pedantry, and wasted effort. One man's pedantry is another man's purism. Take *fruition*. Latinists recognize that it comes from *fruor*, the deponent verb meaning 'I enjoy', and means enjoyment or pleasurable possession. There are examples of this use derived directly from Latin going back to a religious work of 1413 (its spelling having been modernized): 'An Angel hath that knowing of his Creator by very *fruition*.'

The word came to be erroneously associated with the root of *fruit* in the nineteenth century, and abused to mean fruiting or ripeness. (*Fruit* itself is ultimately derived from the Latin *fructus*, meaning the harvest, and connected with *fruor*, *frugi*; perhaps originally meaning to feed on the *fruges* of the earth.) For example, *Harper's Magazine* asserted in 1885: 'The greenish nuts ripened and now in their full *fruition*.' The *OED* described this use as a common blunder. *Webster* and the other American dictionaries of the nineteenth century also refused to countenance this use.

This secondary, fruity usage of the word has now become standard, especially in transferred and figurative senses, and is so recognized by the *OED Supplement* and *Webster's Third New International Dictionary* of 1971. For instance, *The Times* in 1959 wrote: 'This process has now reached full *fruition* with the standardization of body shells for a whole range of models.' The Thunderer was discussing motor cars, not flesh and blood models used to advertise them. Fields are said to need rain for *fruition*: a use that illustrates clearly the mistaken association with *fruit*. Even more commonly the word is transferred to mean realization, accomplishment, or conclusion. So we read of the *fruition* of a far-sighted policy, and learn that somebody has carried a mission to a successful *fruition*.

It is no use purists and Latinists kicking against the pricks. *Fruition* is firmly established in its 'erroneous' meaning, and serves a useful purpose that is not quite served by any other word, including ripeness. To use it in its original sense, for which 'enjoyment' is available as a pretty precise synonym, is likely to be misunderstood and considered pedantic. *Fruition* has won its citizenship and right to a new job.

Other new words and new meanings are less firmly established, and their case for a work permit or a change of employment is still undecided. *Inchoate* means incipient, immature, or just beginning, as in (1534): 'No painter should finish that part of Venus which *inchoate* and begun Appeles left off imperfect.' It is often misused to mean amorphous, incoherent, or disorganized, perhaps because things that are just beginning tend, like the earth, to be without form and void. There may also be a back-to-front popular etymological analogy with chaos. Which sense will prevail, or will they continue to coexist side by side? Both jobs are better done for everyday purposes by simpler words like new (or incipient) and disordered (or amorphous). Therefore it would seem sensible to allow such a learned word as *inchoate* to preserve its scholarly meaning uncorrupted. But sense has little to do with the ceaseless ebb and flow of words and meanings.

13 / GAY

A queer use of an inoffensive little word

It has recently become impossible to describe our cheerful and lively friends as *gay* without risk of being misunderstood. For some time longer it has been impossible to describe our eccentric and funny friends as queer without risk of being misunderstood. *Gay* is a friendlier, less hostile epithet for our homosexual friends than queer, and it has established itself, though it is a paradox that it has been expropriated by one of the sadder groups in society. The old meaning survives in the noun, gaiety; and perhaps in the old Suffolk dialect in which *gays* mean the pictures in newspapers, magazines, and picture-books. It is queer that such an inoffensive old three-letter word, for which there is no exact synonym, should have acquired a wholly new meaning and dropped its old one so rapidly.

The earliest use of the new sense recorded by the *OED Supplement* is in a book of English underworld and prison slang published in 1935, which defined 'geycat' as a homosexual boy. In fact the use is considerably older than that. *Gay* had started to acquire a new sexual meaning by early Victorian times, when it was used to mean that the person so described was either promiscuous, or actively engaged in prostitution. The earliest use of the word in this sense seems to have been about 1840. In his *Dictionary of Historical Slang*, Eric Partridge gives '*gay* house', as meaning a brothel; '*gay* girl', meaning a prostitute; and 'feel *gay*', meaning to feel amorous. All his examples date from around 1870.

This equivocal usage of *gay* may have come from the French. The verses that got Pierre Jean de Béranger (1780-1857), the author of very popular light verse *chansons*, into trouble included:

'*Gai, Gai*, l'on est chez nous
Toujours en fête,
Et cul par dessus tête.
Gai, Gai, l'on est chez nous,
Toujours en fête et par dessus dessous.'

34

But the offence taken was probably as much political as moral.

The documents of the Cleveland Street Scandal of 1889, which were opened to public scrutiny by the Public Record Office in the summer of 1975, give the first example so far found of *gay* meaning homosexual. This famous and purulent Victorian scandal arose from a male homosexual brothel patronized by some of the highest in the land, who applied powerful pressure to have the scandal hushed up. One of the chief witnesses in court was an earnest young man called Saul, a male prostitute, who referred to himself and his colleagues as *gay* in depositions made to the police. There is no evidence that he was in jocular mood.

From England the use seems to have crossed the Atlantic, so that in 1955 Peter Wildeblood in his apologia, *Against The Law,* could define *gay* as 'an American euphemism for homosexual'. Over the past decade the new use has grown from coy euphemism to accepted slang as both adjective and substantive, as in *Gay Liberation.*

This interesting process has created possibilities of *double entendre* and other confusion. It is now difficult to use the old cliché, 'with *gay* abandon', or to say, 'It's a *gay* day', without sounding like Larry Grayson at his most leery. Neither of these is a great loss. The sub-editor who splashed 'Arsenal Go *Gay*' in big type all over the sports pages of the *Evening Standard* at the end of the 1976 football season was inviting, and no doubt received, ribald rejoinders from Highbury. All those sentimental pop songs of the Edwardians and the Twenties, in which *gay* was almost as much a key word as moon and June and love, have taken on ambiguous new connotations; though, in view of the disreputable Victorian past of the word, they may not have been entirely free from alternative interpretation, even when first performed. The 'bachelor *gay*' in the old ballad was a randy hetero.

The prominent American golfer, *Gay* Brewer, may attract some funny looks in the locker-room these days. The French diplomat who in 1918 made the comment to Sir Thomas Beecham on modern dancing: 'Their faces are so sad, but their bottoms are so *gay*', would need to rephrase his remark today, or risk being grossly misunderstood. The enchanting light musical film of 1934, *The Gay Divorce,* starring Fred Astaire and Ginger Rogers, would have to change its title today, or risk prosecution under the Trade Descriptions Act. That entertaining biographical novel about the life and loves of Robert Burns, entitled *The Wonder Of All The Gay World,*

35

now throws a new and entirely spurious light on the career of that ardent heterosexual. It would be difficult today to use the nineteenth-century nursery rhyme as it was used in the House of Lords in 1948 to congratulate Princess Elizabeth, as she then was, on the birth of the Prince of Wales:

> 'The child that is born on the Sabbath day
> Is fair and wise, and good and *gay*.'

The popular Soho restaurant, The *Gay* Hussar, has acquired new nominal connotations to go with its admirable goulash.

Professor Nicholas Kurti, Professor of Physics at Oxford, asked after this article was first published whether we are really obliged to give up using a word in its old-established sense just because it has acquired a new meaning. He wrote, with style: 'Doctors and nurses, in giving injections, still refer to the little pricks; plumbers go on repairing or replacing our ballcocks; mechanics go on turning, milling, boring, and screwing; so why should I be misunderstood if I repeat the remark about *The Beggar's Opera* having made *Gay* (the author) rich and Rich (the original producer) *gay*?'

It is, however, too late to resist or regret this transformation of *gay*. It has happened too quickly and spread too widely; and it is no longer possible to use the word unequivocally. Either it will establish itself permanently as the gentle colloquial term for homosexual; or sexual euphemism and slang, which are always prolific and restless for novelty, will pass on to invade some other word. Another generation will then be able to rediscover a short, useful, *gay* word with an old meaning not quite conveyed by any other word.

14/ GRASS ROOTS

*Don't let the grass roots
grow under your feet
or you will end up with a sod*

The *grass roots* have grown so lush in popular political oratory that fastidious listeners to politicians are suffering from hay fever. Unfortunate audiences have recently been introduced to 'a canny *grass rooter*'; a *grassroots* rebellion, which sounds uncomfortably slippery under foot; and a *grassroots* platform, presumably erected upside-down in a subterranean auditorium. This modish metaphor for the rank and file of a political party or for uncommitted voters implies a lofty and patronizing attitude in those who use it. A *grass root* spends its life under ground, being trodden on, visited only by moles, worms, and other low creatures; being periodically cropped, mown, rolled, and grazed over; and fed, if it is lucky, only with liquid droppings of rain and manure from above.

The phrase originated in the United States, at first keeping its down-to-earth rural flavour, implying simple virtues of the land as opposed to city-slicker qualities. It had its own roots in mining terminology, being used by the mining industry in the second half of the nineteenth century to mean the soil just beneath the surface. From there it was adopted as a political metaphor. The earliest recorded use was at the Bull Moose Convention in Chicago in 1912, when the chairmoose said: 'This party comes from the *grass roots*. It has grown from the soil of the people's hard necessities.' The United States Farmer-Labor Party used it as a slogan in 1920, suggesting that the word still retained its agricultural connotations. And the Republicans held what was described as the *Grass Roots* Conference in 1935 in their unsuccessful campaign to defeat F. D. Roosevelt. Now most politicians on both sides of the Atlantic claim to be in touch with and on the side of the *grass roots,* on the same principle that they claim to be against élitism, sin, and death, and on the side of getting elected. In Britain the *grass roots* now appears to mean anywhere more than a mile from Westminster, whether farm land or urban concrete. The *grass roots* have

37

spread a long way from their home in the cornfields of Iowa.

The metaphor was in fact first used by Kipling in a curious passage in *Kim*, published in 1901: 'Not till I came to Shamlegh could I meditate upon the Course of Things, or trace the running *grass-roots* of Evil.' The word here means the fundamental level, the source or origin, or the ramifications, without the political connotations that subsequently accreted to it. Kipling does not explain how his *grass roots* contrived to run. But gardeners take him to have been referring to *Agropyron repens*, the common couch or twitch grass, whose long creeping root-stalks or rhizomes run below the surface, and make it a pestilential and ineradicable garden weed.

The phrase came to be used quite regularly as the century grew older, until *The Times*, still cautiously quarantining it inside inverted commas to indicate that it did not give its whole-hearted imprimatur, could write in 1952: 'Pushkin and Bakunin were only two of many famous men who were given an opportunity to study at leisure what would now be called the *"grass-roots"* of Russian civilization.' There was even a book, *The Grass Roots of Art*, published in 1947, which incorporated the phrase in its title.

Across the Atlantic the political metaphor, used to describe the rank and file of the electorate or of a political party, flourished and still flourishes rankly. The useful little phrase can, like Canon Chasuble's sermon, be adapted to almost any occasion, and has lost its roots in the country. But purists in the United States still use it to make a distinction between the inhabitants of the rural areas, largely prairie, and those of the big cities. *Grass roots* in this strict use signifies the farming and rural districts of a country, as distinguished from the industrial and urban; and, as the sociologists put it, the people of these districts when constituting or acting as a fundamental politico-economic group and a source of independent popular opinion. What urban and industrial voters are taken to be is not reported: spanners or slabs of concrete? British newspapers and politicians do not make this distinction between *grass roots* for the country and the urban electorate, partly because the metaphor is not native in its political application, and partly because the rural areas are electorally far less significant in Britain than in the United States. An ingenious journalist coined the 'rice-roots' as a metaphor for the ordinary electorate of South-East Asia.

The phrase has grown so luxuriantly out of hand that there are regular examples recorded by the magnificently impartial lexicographers (who have to record usages of words whether they approve

38

of them or not) of *grass rooted* being used as a past participle, and *grass rooters* as a noun to describe those who come from the *grass roots,* which are in this use interpreted as a place, not the rank and file themselves. Mercifully no use of *grass root* as an intransitive verb has yet been recorded, but it can only be a matter of time. This excessive and incongruous use has turned a vivid metaphor, gloriously demagogic when originally sown, into very mouldy hay. A stiff dose of selective weed-killer and repeated mowing of his prose are recommended for anybody tempted to use it yet again.

15/ GUERRILLA

Slippery weapons in the war of words

Words about violence and warfare are among the most slippery of value words, as treacherous as the activities that they comment on while purporting to describe. One man's freedom fighter is another man's rebel, who is another man's terrorist, who is another man's murderous, cowardly, and otherwise execrated thug. The only safe bet is that rebels have sometimes had a righteous cause (value judgment), and that when freedom fighters win, those uninvolved in their fight sometimes have their freedom diminished rather than extended (another value judgment).

The adoption of freedom fighter as an honorific description of somebody who takes part in a resistance movement against the established political system of a country is recent. The earliest use recorded by the *OED Supplement* occurs in a poem by John Lehmann published in 1942:

'Their freedom-fighters staining red the snow.'

Poets are still the most influential word-makers and nomenclators, though not many people read poetry.

Equally instructive is the way that rebels, terrorists, and other men of violence try to make their activities respectable by adopting the nomenclature of established armies. So we have the leaders of a handful of lethal and wanton gunboys styling themselves grandly as Chiefs of Staff and Battalion Commanders, even though they do not command enough 'soldiers' to form a cookhouse fatigue. They are playing murderous games; but they also know that 'wars' are won with words as well as bullets in the back.

The insoluble difficulty for those who are not partisans, and wish to be precise while remaining cool, is to find words to describe such activities, which describe without taking sides or commenting. Gunman and bomber are fairly straight descriptive words: too unemotionally descriptive to be favoured in the fantasy world in which those who deserve the descriptions live. Terrorist seems a

40

reasonable description of somebody who seeks to impose his will or satisfy his sickness by inflicting random terror on the public. Terrorists, dressed in their paranoid delusions, naturally prefer to call themselves patriot warriors in a real army. They may even think of themselves as being that.

Partisan is an older word for an irregular fighter. In the original use recorded by the *OED* from 1692 it meant a member of a band of light irregular troops employed on special enterprises. From that it has been adopted to mean something even less regular: a *guerrilla*, or member of a resistance movement. Members of the French Resistance in the last war called themselves the *Maquis*, from the Corsican name for the wild native scrubland of that island: '*Le maquis nourrit le bétail, abrite le gibier, et parfois les bandits.*' General Mihailovitch's partisans in Yugoslavia in the last war called themselves *Chetniks* (from *cheta*, a band).

In such an anarchy of terminology the scrupulous neutral is hard-pressed to keep a cool head and find a precise word. But at least we can try to restrict words about war to their vestigial descriptive meanings, even though the description is now overlaid with layers of accreted emotion and rhetoric. *Guerrilla* or *guerilla* is one such word. It is derived from *guerrilla* with the double 'r', the diminutive of the Spanish word for war. It originally meant a little war in English also, as in: 'a succession of village *Guerillas*—an internecine (*sic*) war between the gamekeepers and marauders of game.' In Spanish a *guerrillero* is the name for somebody who fights in a *guerrilla*, and so it used to be in formal English.

As early as Wellington's dispatches from the Peninsula, however, the word has been personalized by a back-formation from *guerrilla* warfare to mean an irregular fighter in such warfare: 'I have recommended to the Junta to set the *Guerrillas* to work towards Madrid.' The English tampered with the spelling as well as the meaning. *Guerilla* spelled with a single 'r' is four times as common as *guerrilla* with a double 'r' in the citations in the *OED*. When the English adopt a foreign word into the language, they often adapt its spelling; and there is nothing in principle against the practice. However, we might as well prefer *guerrilla* with the double 'r'; partly, as good Europeans, because it conforms to the Spanish and French spellings; and partly because it is more aesthetically appropriate, with its warlike rolling 'r's.

The word wears its connexion with formal war on the sleeve of its Spanish battledress. It is, accordingly, an appropriate word to describe irregulars who are engaged in running warfare, hiding in the *maquis*, setting ambushes, vanishing into thin air, and doing all the other things that *guerrillas* are good at.

It is clearly not an appropriate word to describe random and occasional urban terrorists, or hijackers, or skyjackers (in the vividly descriptive American neologism), or any others who do isolated acts of violence. *Guerrilla* implies that, although the fighter is irregular, fighting is for the present his regular and probably full-time occupation. Carlos may or may not be the Jackal. But he is no *guerrilla*. *Guerrilla* Theatre was a hyperbolical and inaccurate name for what is now more generally called Street Theatre.

Terrorists will, no doubt, continue to call themselves generals, *guerrillas,* and other honourable and grandiose appellations. The rest of us will be wise, in the interests of language as well as of peace, to maintain as many clear distinctions as we can in the muddy and bloody business. Perhaps it is impossible to describe irregular fighters against established authority without declaring our emotional hands. But those who are careful of accuracy will resist being impressed by the press-gangs of either side into their war of words.

16/ HOPEFULLY

Hopefully this use will be seen to be otiose

'The Government intends to introduce legislation to abolish sin, poverty, and death, *hopefully* in the next session.'

This fashionable transatlantic abuse of *hopefully* to mean something like 'it is hoped' is spreading like the plague in pretentious circles wherever English is spoken. It is objectionable for two reasons. First, it is illiterate. *Hopefully* has been pre-empted since the seventeenth century to mean: 'in a hopeful manner; with a feeling of hope'. A snobbish example from a book published in 1639 illustrates the old meaning: 'He left all his female kindred either matched with peers of the realm actually, or *hopefully* with earls' sons and heirs.' You confuse matters by giving the word an entirely new meaning unconnected with its etymology and previous use.

But illiteracy on its own is not a sufficient disqualification; we do not run the English language as a drill-yard for grammarians. Clarity must be the principal criterion in any linguistic question. *Hopefully* should therefore be disqualified because it is ambiguous and obscure, as well as illiterate and ugly. For example, the introductory sentence of this chapter does not make it clear who is doing the hoping: the Government, the writer's informant, the writer himself, those who are against sin, poverty, and death, or everybody. The ambiguity of the new use has turned the sentence 'England will bat *hopefully* after lunch' into an amphibology, a statement that admits of two grammatical constructions each yielding a different sense. It could mean, according to the old sense of *hopefully*, that the England batsmen (and their supporters) will be full of hope; which might be a triumph of hope over experience. In the new sense it could mean that it is hoped that the rain will stop, or the other side will declare, or England will dismiss their opponents' tail-enders, so that they can start batting after lunch. By turning our thumbs down to the new use we are resisting a small erosion of the precision of the English language.

43

Part of the attraction of *hopefully* in its new overcoat of meaning is this very ambiguity and imprecision. It commits the user to no confession of his personal hopes. Any blunt fool can say: 'I hope.' Only an exquisite and cagey *cognoscente* says *hopefully*, with its pretentious implication that more people are doing the hoping than he is prepared to divulge, certainly more than the solitary writer behind his typewriter. *Hopefully* nudges and winks at the reader with 'Well, well, we know' or 'We could, an' if we would'. In the same way journalists tend to write: 'Generally reliable sources in the corridors of power at Westminster', when what they really mean is: 'I hear on the fermented grapevine in Annie's Bar.' The first version sounds more impressive.

Hopefully appears to be an aborted mistranslation of the German word *hoffentlich*, which does indeed mean: 'hopingly, it is to be hoped.' The German word for *hopefully* in its old and correct meaning is *hoffnungsvoll*. The first printed use of it found by the *OED Supplement* (volume two, H-N, 1976) was in the *New York Times Book Review* of 1932. But the first recorded British use was not until 1970.

The aberrant modern use seems to have been widely introduced in the 1950s by sloppy American academics, who may be presumed to have spoken German better than English. Their mistranslation of *hoffentlich* produced the misbegotten *hopefully*; in an analogous way to the literal translation of the German that produced the American idiom: 'What gives?' The superior length, hazy impersonality, and fashionable snob appeal of *hopefully* made it immediately attractive, and it rages like a fever, wherever the pretentious speak and write. Another explanation of the origin of the use is that it is telegraphese, intended to save money on the cables of journalists by running several words together, as in 'Update upsum soonest'.

An old-fashioned prescriptive grammarian would define an adverb as a word that modifies and qualifies an adjective, verb, or other adverb; and accordingly cross out *hopefully* in its new sense because it stands on its own, not modifying or qualifying another word.

However, old-fashioned prescription is unfashionable. And there are exceptions to the rule that even the most pedantic grammarian would have to accept. A number of adverbs have over the years acquired an absolute use similar to the new meaning of *hopefully*; for example, clearly, presumably, apparently, obviously, conceiv-

44

ably, understandably, and sadly. Regret has even got two adverbs: regretfully for the normal adverbial use to qualify some other word with a sense of regret; and regrettably for the absolute meaning 'it is regretted that'. The *Oxford English Dictionary* allows the absolute use of mercifully, justifying it to mean 'through God's mercy'. Its earliest and most exciting example is from 1836: 'Mrs Villiers in galloping to cover was pitched off, but mercifully escaped with life and limb.'

Most of these adverbs that can be used absolutely come from a group classified as adverbs of cognition. One way of explaining their absolute use is to say that they are condensed main clauses introducing dependent noun clauses. 'Apparently/regrettably/conceivably/presumably he has been drinking' can be analysed to 'It is apparent/regrettable/conceivable/to be presumed that he has been drinking'.

It can reasonably be argued that *hopefully* should be admitted to this select band of adverbs that can be used in a condensed and absolute way. And some good grammarians and sensitive users of English do argue that it is arbitrary and inflexible to prohibit *hopefully*; and that it is a useful new meaning that says compendiously what cannot be said so precisely any other way. The *OED Supplement* merely says that the use is avoided by many writers.

The argument for giving thumbs up to *hopefully* should be resisted, because *hopefully* is ambiguous while none of the other cognitive adverbs is; and because its new use is a pompous euphemism for the plainer verb: 'I, we, or they hope; or it is hoped.' Ask any self-important politician when he expects something to happen, and you can risk betting a verbal particle to a volume of the *OED* that his reply will start: 'Hopefully . . .' It is confusing to have the same word doing duty for both 'in a hopeful fashion' and 'it is to be hoped'. Rather than blunt the sharp edge of the language in this way, we should do better to invent a new word, if we must have an adverb to mean 'it is hoped'.

The Germans have two separate words; and so do the Dutch, *hoopvol*, 'in a hopeful fashion', and *hopelijk*, 'I hope that'. The Romance languages manage perfectly well with no adverb to mean 'it is hoped'. It would be clearer if we introduced 'hopably', or 'hopingly', or 'hopedly' (a trisyllable on the analogy of the journalistic neologism 'reportedly', meaning 'it is reported'), and reserved its original meaning for *hopefully*. But a living language ignores the protests of grammarians and the interests of clarity.

If *hopefully* must be established in its new sense, some indication that it is being used absolutely as a periphrasis for 'I hope' can be given by accent and intonation, by putting *hopefully* in its new sense invariably as the first word in its sentence or clause, or by putting commas around it to show its absolute isolation.

Fearfully and dreadfully, the expression is establishing itself and pushing the legitimate fledglings out of the nest. Doubtfully it can be rooted out at this late stage. Presumably Stevenson's 'To travel *hopefully* is a better thing than to arrive' will be unintelligible to a future generation of English-speakers. But it is to be hoped that we can eliminate the new use, and instead say what we mean in plain words, without showing off, looking *hopefully*, though not optimistically, to the future of English usage.

17/ HYSTERIA

A form of paranoia that can cause offence

Psychology, psychiatry, and psychoanalysis are a fashionable trinity of religions of the twentieth century. Their doctrines are widely regarded with superstitious awe, and as widely misunderstood; their formularies and scriptures are being widely adopted as metaphors into the common language. This misunderstanding and usurpation of the latest pseudo-medical jargon is nothing new; cf. what happened to chronic, hectic, sanguine, and phlegmatic. So laymen carelessly use *neurotic* and *psychopath* to describe unpleasant people whom they do not much care for. *Obsessional* is misused to mean no more than meticulous or punctual. *Paranoid* is misapplied to mean suspicious. And all the other muddy jargon of Freudian English, from *ambivalent* and *ego* to *fixation* and *trauma*, is bandied about with more freedom than precision. We blunt the points of words that do not seem always to be very sharp even in their esoteric use.

Hysterical is often used in popular speech to mean little more than feminine. *Trauma* and *traumatic,* in addition to being loosely used, are vulgarly mispronounced to rhyme with 'How now, brown cow?', as if they were spelled with an 'ow' instead of a Greek 'au'. Perhaps they are assumed to be German words because so many good psychiatrists are German. A *neurotic* is a man who builds a castle in the air. A *psychotic* is the man who lives in it. And a psychiatrist is the man who collects the rent. *Claustrophobic* has recently been given an odd transferred secondary meaning, from describing a person suffering a morbid dread of confined places, to describing any confined place that might induce such a dread.

Hysteria is a condition that manifests itself by overaction of some parts of the nervous system, or by failure of other parts to perform their necessary work. As a consequence the victim suffers mental changes, convulsive seizures, spasms and contractions of limbs, paralyses, loss of sensation over areas of the body, affections of

47

various internal organs, derangement of joints, and combinations of these, which closely mimic various organic diseases. The condition is far more common in women than in men.

As the Greek etymology of the word indicates, it used to be supposed that the origin of the disease lay in trouble of the womb. The best modern opinion is that, although sexual disturbances often occur in the condition, they are symptoms rather than causes. *Hysteria* is caused by the unconscious repression of painful or unacceptable emotions, from which the conscious mind dissociates itself. Treatment varies, but includes the admirable prescription, which is more generally applicable than merely to *hysterics* or young women: 'No *hysterical* young woman should remain unoccupied, but should be provided with, and forced to do, some congenial work.' To describe somebody as *hysterical* when you mean no more than over-excited is medically erroneous and personally offensive.

Medical men, particularly psychologists and psychiatrists, are notoriously imprecise and idiosyncratic with their jargon. It therefore behoves the rest of us to be particularly careful when using their jargon figuratively. Otherwise it is easy to fall into hyperbole and absurdity. It is also easy to cause offence to those who really do suffer from the disease.

For example, it is a current vogue to use *schizophrenia* and *schizophrenic* as impressive alternatives for such workaday phrases as 'in two minds' or 'undecided'. A very bad thriller film of 1976 entitled *Schizophrenia* propagated the myth that the left hand of a *schizophrenic* does not know what his right hand is doing. *Schizophrenia* in real life is the technical term for serious forms of psychosis, in which there is a cleavage of the mental functions, expressed colloquially as a split personality. It brings delusional behaviour, dissociation, emotional deterioration, and other dangerous and unpleasant effects. To trivialize the word as a synonym for irresolute is cheap and offensive to *schizophrenics* and their families and friends. Mockery of the afflicted is a primeval herd instinct, but it is not admirable.

The same applies to the current popular misuse of *paranoia* to mean merely a condition of nervousness or suspicion. It is in fact a form of fixed delusional insanity, in which delusions of persecution and grandeur, and the projection of personal conflicts, are ascribed to the supposed hostility of others. To call somebody *paranoid* when he just has a chip on his shoulder, or an over-high esteem of

48

himself, as most of us do at times, erodes the language and mocks serious infirmity. The same is true of the even more cruel slang of the school playground, which uses *moron* to mean silly, and *spastic* to mean stupid or not very athletic.

The most startling recent figurative abuse of a medical term was Sir Harold Wilson's suggestion that Mr Peter Griffiths, who defeated Patrick Gordon Walker at Smethwick in the 1964 general election with a campaign that was described as racialist, should have the Conservative whip withdrawn from him, and serve out the Parliament as a parliamentary *leper*. This was not only offensive, as intended, to Mr Griffiths, who could look after himself. The suggestion that a *leper* has a terrifying, incurable, infectious disease, and should therefore be shunned like the plague by the rest of the community, is medieval, superstitious, medically untrue, and grossly offensive to the 350 patients registered as suffering from leprosy in this country, and the thousands in the rest of the world. The mythology of the ancient scourge of the crusaders, and the old odium attached to the word prevent the eradication of the ugly disease by frightening the *lepers* of primitive communities from co-operating with modern medicine.

These and other medical and psychoanalytical metaphors can be vivid in an occasional judicious context. But their popular use often gravely misrepresents the original meanings of the words, so far as the psychoanalysts can agree among themselves what those true meanings are. It runs the risk of offending those who suffer literally and not metaphorically from the various conditions. And it produces a pretentious and fashionable style.

18/ IMPERIALIST

Imperialist state-pig

As she was removed from court in Stuttgart on 30 September 1975, Frau Ulrike Meinhof, the West German terrorist leader who was found hanged in her cell a few months later, shouted at the judge: 'You *imperialist state-pig.*' This rousing insult is a refutation of the orthodox theory that we moderns do not curse with the imagination and polysyllabic skill of our ancestors; but concentrate instead with dreary repetition on short, sharp, rude words that have turned what more prudish generations called their private parts into our public insults. An *Imperialistische Staatsschwein* is as elaborate and awful an epithet as the complicated medieval invocations of parts of God's body, in the days when blasphemy was shocking, and accordingly performed the cathartic function of swearing. When its separate limbs are dissected, an *imperialist state-pig* turns out to be as curious and instructive a mongrel as a chimera, which had the head of a lion, the tail of a serpent, and the body of, of all things, a goat.

Imperialist has become one of the most widespread and woolly terms of political abuse in the second half of the twentieth century. It serves to denigrate such radically different and consciously opposed political and economic systems as Soviet *imperialism* in Eastern Europe and American economic (dollar, Yankee) *imperialism,* more commonly called neo-colonialism. Yet it started life as an inoffensive descriptive word. It was originally used in English to describe adherents to or the system of the Holy Roman Empire, or the political doctrines that drew on Roman law in order to establish that the king was emperor in his own realm. In the Italian and German wars of the Middle Ages the Ghibellines were *imperialists,* that is, supporters of the Emperor; while the Guelphs were the papal and popular party. The earliest recorded use of the word in English in 1603 exemplifies this purely descriptive use: 'The *imperialists* imputed the cause of so shameful a flight unto
50

the Venetians.' No doubt for a Guelph such as Dante *imperialist* had pejorative connotations.

Imperialism and its cognate words began to acquire pejorative overtones in English and German in the nineteenth century, when they were used to describe adherents of the Bonaparte family, under which the First and Second Empires were set up. Thus *The Times* of 1869 equated *imperialism* with despotism. After the disappearance of the Second Empire in France, *imperialism* with its new Napoleonic and depreciatory connotations passed into the polemics of British party politics. Liberals denounced Disraeli's policies as *imperialism*. With this powerful word they intended to draw a comparison between him and Napoleon III, and to imply that they shared a common lack of principle and appetite for despotism. So *imperialism* came to mean an unprincipled and disreputable desire to acquire possessions overseas. The *Daily News*, a Liberal newspaper, referred in 1898 to 'that odious system of bluster and swagger and might against right on which Lord Beaconsfield and his colleagues bestowed the tawdry nickname of *Imperialism*'.

Early in the twentieth century a number of political writers, the most influential of whom were K. Kautsky, J. A. Hobson, and Lenin, extended the theory of modern *imperialism* as a stage in the development of capitalist economy. In particular they linked this disreputable *imperialism* with the activities of European financiers overseas. This new form of economic *imperialism*, with its implications of indirect political manipulation, is the kind attributed to American and other neo-colonialisms. Soviet *imperialism* is rather the old-fashioned kind of direct political and military government from an *imperial* centre. *Imperialism* has become one of the most potent negative words of modern political discourse, partly because of the Leninist vocabulary of demonology, and partly because of the feelings of ex-colonies about their old masters. The word has accreted such strong overtones referring to fundamental social and political value judgments that its precise descriptive meaning has been eroded. It has become an insult, not a statement.

If *imperialist* has become a Leninist insult with little or no connexion with the original meaning of empire, *state* has an ugly ring of Nazidom. It echoes all those compounds with *Staat*, like the acronym *Gestapo*, from the days when the *state* was one of the prime gods in the Nazi pantheon. The point of *state* as an insult was not that Judge Theodor Prinzing was a public servant, but that he was part of the pandemonium of supposedly demonic enemies, against whom violent revolutionaries direct their aggression.

But the *pig* is the most incongruous element in the chimeric insult. *Schweinhund* is a venerable German insult, as *cochon* is in French. But the usual German pejorative slang for a policeman is *bulle*, a bull. *Pig* is American of the middle and late 1960s, a hostile or insulting epithet used especially by radicals to describe policemen and sometimes other law-enforcement officers. An early example from *The Black Panther Newspaper* of February 1971 is: 'Jake was murdered in a shoot-out in Chicago where three *pigs* were killed and seven wounded.'

The word is gradually being diluted, on the usual pattern of vogue words, to embrace a wider and wider range of enemies. The usage has been adopted and translated by young radicals and revolutionaries around the world, sometimes with spectacular terminological consequences. For example, Frau Meinhof herself, in an article attempting to justify the use of force against the police, wrote: *'Die Bullen sind Schweine'*—'the bulls are pigs'; in which case somebody had better send for a vet rather than a gunman.

This current abusive use of *pig* as a hostile epithet is the re-emergence of an old English expression. *Pig* in this sense was part of London underworld slang throughout the nineteenth century, and probably long before. *The Flash Dictionary* of 1812 defines police-runners as *'Pigs* or Grunters'. During the Second World War *pig* was a general term of disdain applied to naval officers by other ranks in many ships and shore establishments. One reason for this may have been that the gulf between the living conditions of officers and ratings was wider in the Royal Navy than in the other services. The term was, of course, sarcastic: it was the ratings who lived like *pigs*, while the officers, from the scruffiest sub-lieutenant up, were treated like lords.

This instructive piece of slang was one of the pointers to the Labour victory in the general election of 1945. The social conditions that the slang reflected were a contributory cause of that victory.

Frau Meinhof's vehement political insult at her trial was therefore composed of the following odd ideological bed-fellows: a Leninist translation of a descriptive word into a value word; a piece of German officialese with Nazi overtones translated into an insult; and a modern American revolutionary slogan revived from the thieves' kitchens of early nineteenth-century London.

19/ INTERFACE

Let's all gather at the interface

When pagans mocked Christians for the solecisms and barbarisms in the Scriptures, Augustine had a squashingly hippo-episcopal reply: 'A man who is asking God to forgive his sins does not much care whether the third syllable of *ignoscere* is pronounced long or short. What is correctness of speech except the observance of the usage of others, confirmed by the authority of speakers of old?'

Not all conversations are as awesome as the *interface* between sinner and God envisaged by Augustine. On less important occasions, for example in prosody, the scansion of the third syllable of *ignoscere* makes all the difference between a good hexameter and a barbarous tumble, spondee over dactyl. Correctness of speech matters because its absence muddies communication. God, unto whom all hearts be open, all desires known, can get the message through the miasma of incorrect and inadequate words. The rest of us are extremely prone to misunderstanding each other anyway, without muddling matters further by misusing the common currency of words.

A suppurating source of muddle is the misuse of new words, for which there is no established usage confirmed by the authority of speakers of old. *Interface* is a fine example of a popularized technicality that has been widely and loosely adopted as an imposing metaphor in the past few years, without anybody daring to betray ignorance by asking precisely what is meant by it. The technical jargons from which it has been popularized are those of printing, chemistry, and, especially, computer technology; and thence space flight technology. *Interface* is a place where faces meet. It refers to anything that mediates between disparate items: machinery, people, thought. The equipment that makes the computer's work visible to the user is called an *interface*. Like all smart new popularized technicalities, the word has been extended widely,

53

boldly, and metaphorically. So the knowing talk of the *interface* between man and computer, between the scientist and the rest of society, between disparate disciplines, and even between different people; as in: 'Our social services group provides an *interface* for the different specialists concerned with the subject.' For *interface* in that example read 'meeting-place'.

Interface is the place at which two independent systems meet and act upon or communicate with each other, as in the *interface* between engineering and science, between man and machine, or, more loosely, between the known and the unknown. A secondary and narrower meaning is the method by which interaction or communication is effected between independent systems or disparate items, as in an *interface* between a computer and a typesetting machine. 'An eyeball to eyeball *interface*' has been recorded in the United States. This sounds a painful confrontation, particularly if one of the participants was wearing contact lenses. The phrase is absurd because the juxtaposition of eyes and face jerks the dead metaphor of *interface* to incongruous life.

Examples have been recorded in the United States of *to interface* used as both transitive and intransitive verb. Transitively it is used to mean to connect by means of an *interface,* as when *interfacing* a machine with a computer. Intransitively it means either to serve as an *interface* for, or to interact or co-ordinate harmoniously with, or to become *interfaced* with.

The verbal use often seems to mean nothing more than to match, harmonize, or work together smoothly. Thus, space-suits have to *interface* with equipment in the cabin. Man and machine are *interfaced.* Computer technicians *interface* with flight controllers. And companies are offered a chance to *interface* with new products. One of the reasons that the wonderful achievements of the space scientists do not inspire even more wonder than they do is the stultifyingly opaque jargon of their mystery.

As a noun *interface* often seems to signify no more than a meeting-place, common frontier, liaison, dialogue, or point of contact. The adjectives used to qualify it do not illuminate its meaning. Sometimes it is a broad *interface*; sometimes a virtual *interface.* And Sir Bruce Fraser in his revision of Sir Ernest Gowers's *The Complete Plain Words* records the interesting use: 'I find myself sitting on a number of *interfaces.*' This sounds as painful as sitting on the fence with both ears to the ground until the iron enters into your soul. In short, *interface* begins to look suspiciously like a

54

showy new metaphor that is being grossly overworked in order to impress. With luck it will follow the usual pattern by soon beginning to irk from surfeit, and so become a laughing-stock.

20/ INTERNECINE

Intestine trouble that began with Samuel Johnson

For such a learned Latin word, *internecine* has long since suffered a paradoxical fate: it is generally pronounced in an unetymological way; and it has almost lost its Latin meaning. It is now generally taken to mean mutually hostile, particularly involving conflict within a group, as in 'the Labour, or Conservative, or Liberal Party is rent by its customary *internecine* warfare'.

There is no trace of this connotation of Kilkenny-cat reciprocal hostility in the use of *internecinus* or *interneciuus* in Latin literature. It is derived from *internecare*, to kill without exception, slaughter, or exterminate. And in Latin the adjective means fought to the death, of battles; or devastating, of disease; or murderous, of quarrels. The most daring transferred use of the word in Latin is not found until the eighth century AD, when Paul the Deacon wrote of 'an *internecine* will, through which its author was murdered'. The Latin roots of the word are *necare*, to kill, *nex*, violent death, and *nocere*, to injure, originally to put to death. This use of *inter* conveyed no idea of mutuality in Latin: compare *interire*, to perish, *intercidere*, to slay, and *interimere*, to destroy.

Internecine made its first appearance in English as a rendering of the Latin *internecinum bellum* in Samuel Butler's *Hudibras*:

'Th' Aegyptians worshipped Dogs, and for their Faith
Made *internecine* war.'

The word was evidently intended to give its Latin meaning, 'attended with great slaughter'; the editor of 1674 noted in a gloss against *internecine*, 'fierce and zealous'. This passage is evidently an origin of the unscholarly pronunciation, with a long instead of a short 'e' in the penultimate syllable.

Samuel Johnson, of all people, that learned classical scholar and fine writer of Latin, mistook the *inter* to signify mutuality, and defined *internecine* in his dictionary as 'endeavouring mutual destruction'. Later lexicographers faithfully copied Johnson's mistake.
56

Lovers of long words adopted it. And from the nineteenth century the word has come to be used generally in the erroneous Johnsonian sense.

It is too late to do anything to correct Johnson's inveterate mistake now. The word has acquired a prescriptive right to its mistaken meaning by a century of uninterrupted misuse. The English language cannot be regulated so as to avoid offending the susceptibilities of classical scholars. They are free to abstain from the word, if they dislike it. And the original meaning of *internecine* is no great loss. There are plenty of adequate substitutes for its true sense: murderous, sanguinary, bloody, destructive. But it is over-used as an impressive vogue word and a popularized technicality, intended to display the erudition of the user, and in fact doing the opposite. This process is usurping the function of the perfectly good word intestine, which really does mean what *internecine* is ignorantly used to mean. *Internecine* is a blood-stained and violent word, and the blood and violence stick to it even in its new overcoat of meaning. It is extravagant to write about *internecine* political warfare, unless you seriously mean that the politicians are hacking and shooting each other.

Intestine political warfare, however, is a fine and correct old usage, with splendid examples going back to the sixteenth century of battle intestine, and the intestine malice of our own hearts. Unfortunately its use as a noun to mean the guts has corrupted its adjectival meaning. The man who uses intestine in its original meaning, as a protest against *internecine*, runs the risk of bombardment by letters from wiseacres asking him whether he has a belly-ache.

21 / LEAN OVER BACKWARDS

Lean over for a low profile

According to Sir Malby Crofton, leader of Kensington and Chelsea Council in the autumn of 1976, in a letter to *The Times*: the police *leaned over backwards* to maintain a *low profile* at the Notting Hill carnival that ended in riot.

This was a delightfully congruous mixture of vogue metaphors. *Low profile* is Pentagonese, or American defence jargon. A synonym is low silhouette. A tank or other military vehicle that has a *low profile* presents less of a target for binoculars and their concomitant artillery. Figuratively people as well as tanks, guns, and other military hardware can keep a *low profile*, by showing an inconspicuous mode of operation or behaviour, keeping their metaphorical heads down, and generally avoiding attention. John F. Kennedy put the advantages of a *low profile* well to his speechwriter, Ted Sorensen: 'Stay out of sight and you stay out of trouble.'

In the United States the quality has even become a name, and such shrinking violets with a passion for anonymity are called *low profiles*, as in: 'We now have a Government of *low profiles*, grey men who represent no identifiable place, no region, no programme.'

One of the first lessons that an infantryman in the British Army is taught is the correct posture for lying prone to fire his rifle. The sergeant plants his elbows for him, making an equilateral triangle with his breast-bone, positions his body at a sharp angle to the line of fire, and finally raps his heels sharply with his swagger-stick to teach him to flatten his ankles on the ground, so maintaining a *low profile* and avoiding a bullet in the Achilles tendon. In civilian life a *low profile* is a recipe for avoiding trouble and having a quiet life, though not for attaining the glittering prizes.

Bending over backwards would certainly be another way of maintaining a *low profile*, though it is difficult to imagine circumstances in which it would be useful. The absurd idiom has now established

58

itself widely in political language. When a Minister or other politician asserts that he is *bending over backwards* to help some worthy cause, he usually wants to give a general impression of benevolence without going so far as to commit himself to giving any particular help.

There are few situations in real life outside metaphor, except a tug of war, in which *bending* or *leaning over backwards* could conceivably help anybody. The latest and most nonsensical variant is *falling over backwards* to help, intended to sound even more complaisant, which would be as helpful as assistance from the Keystone Kops, though probably less entertaining.

The origin of the absurd metaphor is obscure. Eric Partridge in his 1969 supplement to his *Dictionary of Slang and Unconventional English* could get no closer than that it came into vogue in American English in the late 1920s. He defines it as to try very hard, as in: 'You need not *bend over backwards* to please the children.' The *OED Supplement* offers a plausible explanation for the metaphor, which it agrees originated in the United States, and which it describes as colloquial. By *bending* or *leaning over backwards* a person goes to the opposite extreme, in order to avoid a possible bias; he goes almost too far in the effort to overcome his inclination; he favours his enemies; he *leans over backwards* to avoid his natural tendency to step forwards.

The earliest quotation that the Oxford lexicographers have found is from *Nation*, the New York magazine, in an issue of 1925. It describes a politician *leaning over backwards* in his desire to satisfy Serbian demands: an odd lot those Serbians with their demands. A citation from 1937 gives: 'He is being hypercorrect, *leaning over backward* to be correct'; a vivid image of a canting pillar of correctitude.

As with all vogue phrases, the metaphor falls flat from overuse. In any case the expression is so recent that its literal meaning is still near the surface. This makes it impossible to *bend over backwards* to maintain a *low profile* without falling jackass over wit into absurdity.

22/ LEEWAY

Turning leeway on its beam-ends

A little more than seven-tenths of the surface of the earth is covered with salt water. But even more than that proportion of sea flows through the history of Britain and the veins of true Brits. It is therefore surprising and embarrassing that our use of nautical metaphor is so lubberly.

There is a current colloquial and vogue use of *leeway* to mean a desirable or useful piece of room for manoeuvre or margin of error. This stands the nautical meaning of the word on its beam-ends (a tilt of ninety degrees; a complete reversal is to turn turtle), and vexes ancient mariners. *Leeway* means the lateral drift downwind, that is to leeward, of course made involuntarily by a ship, especially a sailing ship, which is trying not to go downwind. A vessel can make a lot of *leeway* if a strong cross tide is running, or if her keel is not long enough or deep enough to give her a good grip of the water and hold her up to the wind. It can be extremely dangerous. Even when it is not, it is entirely undesirable. There are no circumstances in which it is a good thing.

Yet the word now occurs constantly in landlubbers' generalized discourse as if *leeway* were something to be desired, like a breathing-space. It is used as if it meant a respectable margin for error instead of a damaging failure to adhere to the course intended. If people must put on bogus nautical airs, the correct word for room for manoeuvre or margin of error is 'sea-room'.

There is no objection to the general public adopting the technical jargon of specialized activities, and adapting the meaning in the process. The history of English is a constant process of such misapprehension and popularization of technicalities. But it is objectionable, annoying, and potentially confusing if the popularized meaning is so startlingly different from the specialized meaning. Objectionable or not, *leeway* in its loose new matelot's sou'wester of meaning with its spurious whiff of sea air looks like establishing itself.

By and large is another nautical phrase that has drifted to leeward farther than most popularized technicalities. As a nautical term it means to sail a vessel near the wind but not fully on it; that is, about five points off the wind with the fore-and-aft rig and about seven points with square rig. A course between *by* and *large* is one between close-hauled, close to the wind with the sheets hardened in, and one with the wind abeam or aft. A consistent course of this sort is an easy one for the watch on deck, with none of the hard slog of working to windward, and probably little trimming of sail, since the odd squall can be met by luffing. For helmsmen such courses were a pleasant relief: lack of attention or seamanship did not bring automatic penalty as it would with close-hauled steering or with running free in a seaway. *By and large* meant a course when beginners could learn or old hands take it easy at the helm.

The phrase came ashore as far less emphatic than 'as easy as falling off a log' or 'as easy as shooting fish in a barrel', wherever they came from. As a hazy general phrase it is used to mean: in a general aspect, without entering into details, on the whole, broadly speaking, and all things considered. It is curious that it should have sailed so far from its original meaning. But it has settled down comfortably in its new, not very shipshape berth, and does a useful job and no harm in the world, except to vex old sailors, who need a certain amount of vexation to keep them salty.

The devil to pay is an old seafaring term meaning something very difficult or awkward. The devil refers to the upper outboard strake of an old wooden sailing ship, or the garboard seam nearest the keel. Caulkers called them the devil because there was very little space to get at these seams with a caulking iron, and they were particularly awkward and difficult ones 'to pay'—that is, to fill with pitch after they had been caulked with oakum. When a ship was careened, the garboard seam was not only the most awkward to get at, but also the most difficult to keep above water and caulk, and the wettest. It was the devil to pay in the oakum and hammer it home.

The expression in full was *the devil to pay and no pitch hot*, implying a virtually impossible task; whereas the abbreviated form used by landlubbers is taken as a reference to approaching retribution. The nautical expression may have been confused with proverbs referring to alleged bargains with Satan, and the inevitable payment to be made to him by such as Faustus in the end.

The devil in *between the devil and the deep sea* (sometimes *deep-blue sea*) is also a sailor. A caulker caulking the seam in the upper deck planking next to the ship's waterways had nothing outside this strake to save him from going overboard.

To be *taken aback* is another nautical phrase, whose origin in the great days of sail has faded until it is almost forgotten. What it means at sea, as defined by an old sailor, is: 'When through a shift of wind or bad steerage the wind comes in front of the square sails and lays them back against the masts, instantly staying the ship's onward course and giving her stern way; an accident exceedingly dangerous in a strong gale.' Exceedingly dangerous it sounds, and very likely to happen to any of us who tried to sail something with square sails. But now that the seas are almost empty of the great square-riggers, the popularized technicality preserves the nautical phrase as a vivid and for once entirely apt metaphor.

23 / MAFIA

There are mafiosi under the bed

Whenever two or three are gathered together these days, even for the most innocuous purposes, they run the risk of finding themselves defamed by some commentator as a *Mafia*. Films like *The Godfather* have glamorized and vulgarized the secret and criminal society of exceedingly unglamorous and peculiar people, and turned its sinister name into a jocular vogue epithet. So the name of a society of predatory and ruthless criminals is applied indiscriminately to any secret or exclusive society; to any closed circle or clique; and to any group of people of similar interests or backgrounds prominent or powerful in a particular field or enterprise. There need be no hint of criminality in the association described in the new usage as a *Mafia*, though the description is often, but not invariably, uncomplimentary. John F. Kennedy was said to have filled the White House with an Irish *Mafia*, and the *bon mot* was immediately plagiarized to death by the trampling hoofs of a thousand fashionable hacks.

Sour remarks are passed about 'the contemporary literary *Mafia*', generally by people whose books have been received poorly or with complete critical silence. According to this popular modern usage there are an academic *Mafia*, a mental-health *Mafia*, any number of militant Marxist *Mafias* with different creeds and programmes of impenetrable complication, a modern composers' *Mafia* dedicated to atonality and the production of new noises, a *Mafia* of malcontents among ultra-Tories, ultra-Socialists, and ultra-Liberals, a Labour Party *Mafia*, which is said to be over-sensitive about the TUC, and an Australian *Mafia* at the *Sunday Times*, to name but a few recent discoveries of these sinister secret societies in our midst.

The use accords quite well with one popular but extravagant view of society as a gigantic conspiracy and network of interlocking conspiracies, with *mafiosi* and bugs lurking under every bed. The phrase 'the Establishment' has suffered a similar fate of being de-

63

bauched by what Henry Fairlie, one of its originators, described as 'the whole tribe of professional publicists and vulgarizers who today imagine that a little ill-will entitles them to comment on public affairs'.

The hierarchical society of criminals called the *Mafia* arose in Sicily in the thirteenth century, and has flourished on that island of Persephone for centuries because a succession of despotic foreign governments alienated the native population, and made tolerable even the *Mafia*'s perverted system of private justice. The name comes from a Sicilian dialect word for boldness, bluster, and swagger, probably derived from the Arabic word, *mahyah,* which means boasting. The *Mafia*'s peculiar code of justice is based on *omertà,* the code of silence, which demands humility coupled with a kind of mad machismo that under no circumstances allows a *mafioso* recourse to legal authorities or any degree of co-operation with them. Sicilians and Italians who emigrated to North and South America in the late nineteenth and early twentieth centuries took the *Mafia* along with them in their other less vicious luggage; and in the United States it grew to be the largest and most powerful of the syndicated crime organizations, with a structure and rules very similar to those of its Sicilian prototype. According to the FBI in recent years the organization has taken to calling itself by the nasty little euphemism, *Cosa Nostra.*

There is some hope that the *Mafia* may be dwindling in strength and prestige in the United States, partly because of the disappearance of the old-style godfather bosses, who are seen to be anachronisms and ludicrous as well as evil, and partly because Italian-Sicilian culture is at last emerging from its ghettos and becoming assimilated into the larger American society. There is some evidence also that the *Mafia* is declining in Sicily, though any organization that has lasted for seven centuries has deep roots. Land reform after the last war weakened its hold on the rural areas of central and western Sicily, and the *Mafia* has moved its attention on to industry, business, commerce, and building enterprises in the urban areas.

Its nefarious name thrives, however, as a flabby catchword which is rapidly losing all its strong flavours and coming to mean no more than a clan. May the *Mafia* itself shrink into vacuity like its name!

24/ MAJOR

The massive change from major to minor

Adjectives of magnitude and importance are insidious temptations to poor hacks in the communication industries. The temptation is to exaggerate the size or importance of what we are describing, in order to grab the attention of our readers or listeners. Such magnification of epithets is particularly prevalent in advertising: it is one of the commonest and most disreputable tools of the trade. When the evening newspaper billboards blaze forth 'Famous Film Star Dead', it is a safe bet that the film star will be either unknown or so obscure as to be almost invisible to the naked eye. When a really famous film star dies, there are no comets seen on the billboards: the name by itself is a more attractive advertisement: 'Marilyn Monroe Dies'.

A favourite vogue word for saying, 'Listen, look, this is important and significant', is *major*. That fastidious and learned Wagnermane, Bernard Levin, made well-deserved mockery of the improbable military hero of a *Major* Wagner exhibition in 1976. *Major* is the comparative of the Latin *magnus,* and accordingly means greater. It is properly used when there is a clear distinction between *major* and minor: as in musical keys, prophets, canons, diameters, planets, terms, premisses, axes, and homonymous schoolboys. Smith *Major* is so called to distinguish him from Smith Minor, and, if necessary, Smiths Maximus and Minimus. *Major* epilepsy is so named to differentiate it from *petit mal.*

It would indeed be pedantic to insist that *major* should be used only where 'greater', 'rather great', or 'too great' can be substituted for it. It is useful to be able to describe as *major* things of more than ordinary importance, or things likely to have unusually serious consequences, or things that are considerable and principal in relation to things that are negligible and minor. We refer to *major* wars (not tribal skirmishes), *major* accidents (causing many deaths), *major* roads, and *major* powers (a little lower than the superpowers,

65

but a great deal more powerful than the present state of Great Britain).

To speak of a *major* storm in a municipal parks committee, an obscure pop group, or some other teacup, is to invite derision. The harmfulness of the current vogue for *major* as a magnifying epithet is that it saves us the trouble of finding a more precise, less fashionable word such as main, important, significant, chief, principal, or big; or, often more effectively, eschewing any adjective.

Massive is another vogue magnifier that is supplanting more suitable words in the newspapers and broadcasting. Literally it means forming or consisting of a large mass; having great size and weight, or solidity. Transferred and figuratively it is a useful and expressive word for describing immaterial things that are solid, substantial, and great or imposing in scale. But it deserves to be used with discretion and discrimination, or it is devalued. Language thrives by metaphor and figurative extension, and would be impoverished by a ban on the imaginative use of descriptive words. It would be silly to quibble about a painting being described as brilliant on the grounds that it emitted no physical light, or dull on the grounds that light is something that we need to see paintings by, and ought not to expect to derive from them.

Some things that have no connexion with mass, like indiscretions, consort happily with the epithet *massive*. *Massive* indifference has become a cliché. Here *massive* is being used as a near synonym for notable or monumental, to mean impressive or imposing in extent or depth. It is also used to mean imposing through moral or intellectual excellence or grandeur, as in 'a *massive* intellect'. But when P. G. Wodehouse wrote, on the subject of one of his sabre-toothed and pachydermatous aunts, 'A *massive* silence prevailed in the corner where the aunt sat', he was using the adjective humorously. A master of English style can get away with bold metaphors that we who are not masters would be prudent to avoid. In any case, it was Bertie Wooster speaking.

To describe somebody as the most *massive* American dramatist of his time was an unfortunate choice of metaphor, especially since the man in question was skinny, with a lean and hungry look. To describe anybody as a *massive* figure, however important and great he or she may be, is to run the risk of reawakening the literal sense of *massive*, which dozes near the surface of the word, to ludicrous effect.

Heavy is another *heavily* overused magnifier, particularly in the

66

jargon of economic crisis, which has become so prominent a part of the language in the past few years. Thus we have *heavy* unemployment, *heavy* gains, *heavy* losses (for example, on the Stock Exchange), *heavy* increases, *heavy* reductions, *heavy* compensation, *heavy* cut-backs on public (that is to say, more precisely, less euphemistically, Government) expenditure, a *heavy* rise in public (that is, Government) expenditure, *heavy* demands (for example, for gilt-edged stock), *heavy* security precautions, and even a *heavily* orchestrated public relations campaign. Such overuse depreciates the value of useful words. It deserves the *major, massive,* and *heavy* opposition of all who care for the language and wish to keep it precise for the good of everyone.

25/ NECESSARILY

Necessity is the mother of invention,
but it ain't necessarily so

Necessarily is a very strong word that is being weakened by careless vogue use. It implies the irresistible action of causality or logic. If we say that a thing *necessarily* happens, we have in mind the inevitability of its happening. All men are mortal; Socrates is a man; therefore, *necessarily,* Socrates is mortal. Two and two *necessarily* make four in the decimal arithmetic that is generally used in the world of counting. Careless writers and talkers are increasingly tending to use this strong, specialized adverb in contexts that have no tinge of necessity. It is especially popular with writers and orators of opinion, argument, and rhetoric.

You meet this new use in unexpected places: for example, in the leader columns of the newspaper whose leaders are generally agreed to be the most thunderous in opinion and most elegant in style in the English language: 'The Pope's action in . . . is not *necessarily* wrong.' Well, of course not; it would be illogical if it were. Such political and moral actions are governed by empirical value judgments, not by the necessity of causality or logic. The actions of even the most immoral and injudicious of the medieval popes would be *necessarily* wrong only if you made the category mistake of thinking that ethical value judgments were necessary laws like the rules of logic and mathematics. The Pope's action may have been wrong. It may have been imprudent. It may have been contrary to the teachings of the Church and the Bible. But it cannot have been *necessarily* wrong. What the Thunderer seems to mean in its leader is that the Pope's action may or may not be wrong. The writer does not know, cannot make up his mind, or is not at present prepared to say. To use the qualifier *necessarily* in this sense is either evasive, or pompous, or both.

Another pompous imprecision that is particularly attractive to writers of opinion is the use of *more or less* in contexts where either 'more' or 'less' is meaningless. 'A little *more or less* than a ton of

68

red herrings' is correct and intelligible. The phrase is nearly equivalent to 'about a ton' of the elusive fish.

From this correct and intelligible usage *more or less* is coming to be accepted as an impressive synonym for 'about', 'approximately', or 'nearly', even in cases where the object quantified is by nature at the upper or lower limits of the possible range. In such a case either 'more' or 'less' is nonsense, with no *more or less* about the epithet. For example: I arrived *more or less* promptly. How, even with angel's wings, can I arrive one microsecond more promptly than promptly? 'The balance of payments deficit was *more or less* zero.' Apart from being so improbable as to be economic Utopianism, that sentence is nonsense. How can a deficit be less than zero? Well, by becoming a surplus. But the idea of a deficit less than zero is an apparent paradox that causes the reader to stumble. And readers forced to pick themselves up, go back, and go over the jumps of a sentence a second time tend to lose patience and find something less demanding to read.

The motive for these hazy extended uses of both *necessarily* and *more or less* seems to be the common one among writers of opinion: to qualify their bare opinion, both as a safety-net in case they are wrong, and as a politeness, so as not to sound offensively dogmatic. That may be a commendable motive. But good intentions are wasted if they lead to writing nonsense.

26/ OBSCENE

Suddenly everything seems obscene these days

In his hilarious evidence at the *Inside Linda Lovelace* obscenity trial in 1976, Johnny Speight, begetter of Alf Garnett, declared upon oath that he found *Mein Kampf* by Adolf Hitler *obscene*. At first hearing it was a surprising adjective to use about that most unreadable and unread of best sellers. The anthologists are hard put to it to select a single memorable quotation from *Mein Kampf* to include in their dictionaries of modern quotations. Of course, determined obscenity-hounds can sniff out obscenity in every book yet written, except possibly the telephone directory. But until now it had been supposed that *Mein Kampf* ran the telephone directory close, with its boring, repetitive, and rambling rubbish about racial purity and other topics. If prudish Adolf had put in a bit of obscenity, he might have made his book more entertaining; but he would have outraged his deeply respectable petit bourgeois nature and his tight sexual repressions.

Presumably what Johnny Speight meant was that *Mein Kampf*, by signposting for those few who had the patience to read it the road to world war and genocide, was an evil, hateful, and morally outrageous book, perhaps the most abominable ever written: and quite right too. What has happened is that the scope of *obscene* has been rapidly extended in the past few years from its once narrow meaning connected with lewdness and sexual indecency to embrace anything that is morally offensive.

In February 1976 the Archbishop of Canterbury, unable to resist the most widely used pejorative adjective of the decade, denounced 'golden handshakes' to redundant businessmen as *obscene*. This provoked Mr Walter Clegg, the witty Member of Parliament for North Fylde, to puzzle over why the payment of heavily taxed compensation to businessmen who have been unfairly dismissed or made redundant should be described archiepiscopally as an obscen-

70

ity, when Parliament had just voted a right of compensation, sometimes running into thousands of pounds, to any worker who is unjustly sacked. He suggested: 'It would be nice for laymen like myself to be told at what point the payment of compensation becomes *obscene*: in these days of inflation perhaps the going rate could be announced weekly from the pulpit, and perhaps each year in *Crockford's Directory* there could be published an obscenity table, which would set out the point at which the salaries, wages, profits, or stipends earned by people became *obscene*. In that way we could adjust our morals accordingly.'

The present legal definition of obscenity fails because it relies upon two value words almost as slippery as *obscene* itself: deprave and corrupt. And the very search for such a definition is intrinsically a wild-goose chase, if you will pardon the obscenity. In monolithic societies of the past with generally accepted Christian moral values, or of the present with generally accepted totalitarian values, people knew where they were, more or less. In today's fragmented and divided democratic societies one man's obscenity is another man's mild slang, is another man's favourite word, is another man's fuddy-duddy circumlocution. The only hope of a watertight legal definition of obscenity is one that uses descriptive words such as 'children' or 'animals', instead of emotive value words about which there can be no general agreement.

There are people today who find nothing *obscene* in anything to do with their sexual and excretory parts and functions. So the strong word has been extended to describe things like poverty and hunger that modern sensibility finds more offensive than sexual aberration. And so we get the pornography or obscenity of violence; and we find people saying 'the debate was almost *obscene* in its irresponsibility', or '*Mein Kampf* is *obscene*'; and we understand what they are getting at.

The word *obscene* comes from the Latin adjective *obscenus,* which was probably originally and primarily a term of augury, meaning 'boding ill' or 'unpropitious'. From there it developed in Latin the secondary meaning: 'exciting disgust by its unwholesomeness, filthy, polluted, loathsome'. From there it came to be applied in Latin to the sexual and excretory parts and functions; and thence it got the modern English meaning of 'indecent, *obscene,* lewd'. It came into English in the late sixteenth century, probably, like so many Latin words, by way of French. The first instance recorded by the *OED* comes from Shakespeare's *Richard II,* and

71

shows the meaning of 'abominable and loathsome' rather than the derived modern meaning of 'indecent':

'That in a Christian climate souls refined
Should shew so heinous, black, *obscene* a deed.'

The *OED* describes this meaning as 'now somewhat archaic'. But the archaic sense lingered on. In *Our Mutual Friend* Dickens wrote: 'Lightwood stared at the *obscene* visitor.' The visitor in question, Mr Dolls, is obviously morally offensive, or perhaps, by a Latinism, ill-omened, rather than lewd or sexually indecent. But the dominant modern sense of *obscene,* until its recent vogue and rogue extension, has been lewd and indecent.

By a linguistic paradox 'vice' has moved in exactly the opposite direction to *obscene.* From having formerly been of general application, it is now largely used to refer to sexual matters, as in Vice Squad, and vice scandal in the newspaper headlines. 'Vicious', however, has not kept pace with its noun in this shift of meaning, otherwise we could simply adopt 'vice' and 'vicious' to replace *obscenity* and *obscene.* Similarly *obscenity* has not kept pace with *obscene,* but retains a more specific connotation of lewdness, so preventing the other swap of 'vice' for *obscenity.* 'Pornography' is another member of the confused family of moral value words that are shifting meaning fast and erratically, as in 'the pornography of hatred'. Hatred of women or anything else is not included in the primary meaning of pornography. But that is the way the word is being shifted. The trouble about most of these words to do with the seamy side of sex is that we use them loosely to express anger and moral disapprobation. They are becoming mere empty expletives.

This extension and consequent blunting of the cutting edge of *obscene* is linguistically a pity; as is any such process that makes an originally sharp word less precise, and consequently less useful. But luckily such vogue words of rhetoric and political argument tend to lead short, furious lives, until they are driven out by the need for an even more emphatic word of condemnation. There is a devaluation of words as well as of currency. When everything evil is described as *obscene,* there is no particular sting left in obscenity. When the mob that uses words with more heat than precision has passed on to a new fashion, then perhaps *obscene* can revert to its original modest meaning—if by then there is any occupation left for a word to describe what is indelicate and offensive to modesty.

27 / OLYMPICS

Making errors of Olympian size

The English have been giving odd new meanings to old words for centuries. According to Boswell, Samuel Johnson 'was much offended at the general licence by no means modestly taken in his time, not only to coin new words, but to use many words in senses quite different from their established meaning, and those frequently very fantastical'. Every four years when the modern *Olympic* Games, that international festival of chauvinism and bad sportsmanship, come round again, the newspapers and sound-waves are full of fantastical abuses of *Olympic* terms.

This is a different point from the one that the modern games bear little relation to the ancient religious festival at Olympia in Elis that is supposed to be their inspiration. An ancient Greek would have found the presence of women at the *Olympic* Games as spectators, far more as competitors, blasphemous. He would have considered most of the events not games at all, particularly those involving teams and points awarded by judges. The fierce national rivalries and the awards of gold medals and other more valuable concealed benefits to winners would have seemed barbaric.

However, to attribute starry-eyed idealism and pure amateurism to the ancient *Olympics* errs on the side of charity rather than realism. On one occasion the states of Elis and Athens combined to exclude all the Spartan athletes, supposedly on religious grounds, in much the same way that modern nations combine to exclude others or boycott the games on political grounds. And Herodotus tells an instructive story of an Egyptian potentate who gave his opinion that it was unfair that Elis, the host town, should compete, because of her privileged status.

But an inhabitant of Hellas would have found the modern terminology barbaric, even if he found some of the politics and other skulduggery familiar. In modern idiom *Olympic* is the adjective of Olympia and of the games held there and named after

73

it. *Olympian* is the adjective of Mount Olympus, the residence of Zeus and the other Greek gods. Hence it has come down to earth to mean either splendid, or condescending, or indifferent, or supremely calm and dispassionate. This is a useful distinction, though not as old as Shakespeare and Milton. If it is preserved, the headline above this chapter contains an error of Himalayan size.

An *Olympiad* is widely used as an impressive synonym for a celebration of the modern *Olympic* Games. According to the examples in the main text of the *OED*, Sir Ernest Gowers, and other eminent authorities, it actually means the period of four years from one celebration of the Olympic Games to the next. This was the method by which the ancient Greeks computed time, the year 776 BC being taken as the first year of the first *Olympiad*, and the last *Olympiad* beginning in AD 393, and never yet having been completed because of the Dark Ages and other unsporting intrusions.

Unfortunately this useful distinction is not soundly based in either ancient Greek or old English usage. The 1933 *Supplement* of the *OED* gives an example from 1907 of *Olympiad* being used to refer to a celebration of the modern *Olympic* Games. Many earlier examples of *Olympiad* being used to mean the actual games, not the interval between them, can be found and will be recorded in the next volume of the *OED Supplement*. For instance, John Skelton (in about 1490) wrote of Hercules founding tournaments which were called *Olympiades*. Sir Walter Ralegh, in his *History of the World* (1614), surveys the *Olympiad* system of chronology, fixes its starting date, and continues: 'Thus much may suffice concerning the time wherein these *Olympiads* began.' Newton, in *The Chronology of Ancient Kingdoms Amended* (1734), wrote: 'This Breviary seems to have contained nothing more than a short account of the Victors in every *Olympiad*.' And Grote, *History of Greece* (1852), wrote: 'They revenged themselves by pronouncing the 104th *Olympiad* to be no *Olympiad* at all.'

In Greek the adjective *Olympias* was used first by Herodotus, to mean an *Olympic* festival, or, less frequently, an *Olympic* victory. The secondary meaning of the period of four years between one celebration of the *Olympic* Games and the next is not found until about 150 years later. It was probably introduced in the early third century BC by Timaeus, the first historian to use the *Olympiad* framework for chronology. The dualism of the Greek usage slips

74

quite easily between the two meanings. It would be convenient to establish a distinction in English by reserving *Olympiad* for the chronological quadriennium, especially since its use to mean the *Olympic* Games themselves seems to be inspired by the tawdry wish for elegant variation. However, it is not possible to say that the latter use is wrong.

To give the ancient and sacred title of *Olympics* to trivial international contests other than the *Olympic* Games is barbarous vulgarity, and blunts the language. No doubt bridge seems an interesting and even important game to addicts. But to stage Bridge *Olympics* is to debase Olympia and make bridge appear a ridiculous parvenu. What is wrong with calling a spade a spade, and an international championship an international championship?

Marathon is widely abused figuratively to mean any feat of endurance, so that we have had dancing, coaching, piano-playing, and even potato-eating *marathons*. The point about the original *marathon* was speed rather than keeping on going until everybody else gave up. When the Persians landed at *Marathon* in 490 BC the Athenians sent Pheidippides, their fastest runner, to Sparta to ask for help. He made the round trip of 150 miles in two days flat, pausing only for a conversation with the god Pan, who wanted to know why the Athenians did not worship him. It was a wasted journey, since the Spartans made the excuse that for religious reasons they could not set out to help before the full moon.

After the Athenians had miraculously defeated the Persians at *Marathon* without Spartan reinforcements, they sent their fastest runner, presumably Pheidippides again, to carry the good news to Athens, whose non-combatant citizens were waiting anxiously, expecting the worst. He took the main road from *Marathon* running south of Mount Pentelicus to Athens, a distance of about twenty-six miles. Having gasped out the news of the great and unexpected victory, he dropped dead in the Agora.

No doubt much of the story is legendary. The legend of a runner who brings news of a great victory or defeat and then falls dead from exhaustion is found elsewhere in mythological chronicles. But to use *marathon* to describe any trivial feat of endurance, such as playing the piano non-stop for longer than anybody else in order to make a paragraph in *The Guinness Book of Records,* is vulgar and inaccurate. The object of the original *marathon* was to get somewhere as quickly as possible, not to spend as long as possible on the way.

The precise distance of the modern *marathon* was fixed at 42.195 kilometres (26 miles 385 yards) at the 1908 *Olympic* Games of the fourth modern *Olympiad* held in London. This was the distance from where Queen Alexandra, sitting in the shade in the lower ward of Windsor Castle, started the *marathon*, to the finishing line at the White City stadium. The race was memorable because Dorando Pietri, the little Italian who finished first, was disqualified because he had collapsed from exhaustion on the final lap inside the stadium and had been revived by doctors. Queen Alexandra presented him with an enormous gold cup as a consolation prize, in a gesture that expressed the feelings of most spectators. The race is still memorable, because the arbitrary decision of where Queen Alexandra should sit to keep out of the sun fixed for future *marathons* the exact distance that Pheidippides is supposed to have run from *Marathon* to Athens twenty-five centuries ago.

28/ PARAMETER

Black sheep among the statistics

The recent virulent epidemic of hyperparametritis (addiction to the use of *parameter*; not the medical term parametritis, meaning a painful inflammation of the tissues around the womb) shows no signs of abating within the so-called *parameters* within which the pretentious write and speak. In 1976 the Lord Chief Justice commented from the austere purity of his bench: '*Parameter*: a word, I may say, that has been much abused in this case.' An international organization recently recorded on its list of standing committees 'a committee on *parameters* of interface', a piece of UNESCOspeak gibberish that is a strong candidate for the title of obfuscation of the year.

The revised edition of Gowers's *The Complete Plain Words* (1973) crisply defined *parameter* as: 'A mathematical term with a precise meaning which, it is safe to say, not one in ten of those who use it understands.' The number now seems nearer to one in a hundred, many of the ninety and nine black sheep appearing to confuse the word with perimeter.

Parameter is a technical term of various branches of higher mathematics and statistics. It has been widely adapted as a popularized technicality, evidently because it confers a spurious but impressive air of mathematical exactitude on less exact subjects such as sociology, politics, and economics.

Higher mathematics are deep waters, Watson, likely to engulf all but the strongest swimmers. But here follow the principal meanings attached to *parameter* by those who use the word reverently, discreetly, advisedly, soberly, and in the fear of God, and considering the causes for which *parameter* was ordained. These are:

1. In conic sections: the third proportional to any given diameter and its conjugate (or, in the parabola, to any abscissa on a given diameter and the corresponding ordinate).
2. In mathematics (specifically, the Theory of Functions, and

77

thence calculus): a quality which is constant in a particular case considered, but which varies in different cases; especially a constant occurring in the equation of a curve or surface, by the variation of which the equation is made to represent a family of such curves or surfaces.

3. In astronomy: the data necessary to determine the orbit of a heavenly body.

4. In crystallography: each of the intercepts made upon the axes in a crystal by the plane which is chosen for the face of the unit or primary pyramid.

5. In analysis of contemporary music: the musical boundaries of the particular piece. These *parameters* do not bind the composer in any other composition: for example, the *parameters* (such as highest and lowest notes, longest and shortest notes) of Stockhausen's Piano Piece Number One do not establish the *parameters* of Piano Piece Number Two.

6. In medical writing: any measurement made on a patient. Thus, in a clinical study, the investigator may state that he observed ten *parameters* for each patient. Statisticians frown on this use, and would prefer their own jargon 'variable' or 'variate'.

7. In statistical theory: a quantity which determines the distribution of a random variable, and which can be estimated from sample data.

8. In unspecialized discourse, as a snob's yardstick: usually no more than a grand and showy substitute for boundary, limit, framework, or condition; any defining or characteristic factor, as in: 'Still, by the *parameters* that count, I am among the more liberated women in my zip code.'

Scientists are accustomed to non-scientists adopting their technical terms (for instance, 'force' and 'energy'), and giving them looser meanings in ordinary conversation. However, it is disturbing to find a word used with different meanings in so many different scientific disciplines.

The statistical meaning, number seven in the above list, is probably responsible for the popularization of *parameter* as an impressive vogue technicality, statistics being a fashionable study, prolific of jargon that has the ring of mathematical certitude. Those who use *parameter* would help their audience to understand them if they were to indicate in which of its senses they wished the word to be understood. In ninety-nine cases out of a hundred it would prove to be meaning number eight.

78

29/ POPULIST

A touch of populist and demagogic tradition

Populist (and its generic class of politics, *populism*) have recently been adopted as vogue words in British political discourse to put down policies as diverse as those of Tony Wedgwood Benn and Enoch Powell. It is usually a mildly derogatory epithet: meaning something like anti-élitist, pro the little man against his paternalist masters in Whitehall, and appealing to simple fear and greed. An extremely *populist* programme would be one to halve taxes, double social benefits, reintroduce capital punishment, and give every voter a 'free' gallon of beer on the Prime Minister's birthday.

Populist has an interesting history, and consequent historical connotations that differentiate it from 'demagogic' and 'popular', with which in this country it is often confused as a supposedly elegant variation. Its origin lies in American politics, that rich compost heap of political language.

In the nineteenth century periodic depressions and the belief that the United States Government was run principally for the benefit of big business led to informal alliances between farmers, manual workers, and socialists. In 1890 a state party calling itself the People's Party or the Party of the People was founded in Kansas. In the same year farmers' alliance groups, founded largely to fight the railroads, did extremely well in elections in the South and West. Accordingly in 1891 a national *Populist* Party or Party of the People was organized. At its convention in Omaha it agreed on a radical programme that included: nationalization of the railways, telephones, and telegraphs; direct election of United States Senators; limitation of the private ownership of land; a graduated income tax; and cheaper money, achieved by free coinage of silver and increased issue of paper money. Its manifesto called for 'a permanent and perpetual union of the labor forces of the United States', and asserted: 'The interests of rural and civic (sc. urban) labor are the same, their enemies are identical. We believe that the time has come

79

when the railroad corporations will either own the people, or the people must own the railroads.'

In the 1892 presidential election the *Populist* candidate, General James B. Weaver, won twenty-two electoral college and 1,029,846 popular votes. Many people, including some who called themselves liberal, thought that red revolution was about to engulf them. Capitalists shivered, and removed their money to Europe. But the *populists* faded away almost as fast as they had crawled out from the grass roots. The party lingered on until 1908, but by then most of its members had returned sheepishly to the Democratic fold.

The Russian Narodnik *Populist* Party, a socio-political movement advocating a form of collectivism and a policy of 'Go to the People' from 1874 onwards, was another source of the general use of the word, but not such an influential one as the American.

In the United States the epithet *populist* has now had its precise point blunted to mean somebody who purports to represent the rank and file of the people, with connotations of the old-fashioned radicalism of American history. Lyndon Johnson was described, not entirely aptly, as a political leader in the old *populist* tradition.

Whether it is an insult or a compliment to be called a *populist* depends upon who is speaking and his tone of voice. It is certainly a politer word than demagogue, which is almost always depreciatory. However, even demagogue can be commendatory in some contexts. George Steevens, the journalist, wrote in 1897 : 'In a free country every politician must be something of a demagogue. Disraeli and Gladstone were both finished demagogues, and until we have two more great demagogues in England, politics will continue to be as dishwater.' Eventually Lloyd George filled the gap.

Populist is a useful addition to the British English vocabulary of politics, so long as we do not quite forget its historical roots, and so long as we remember that those who shout the loudest for the people in the abstract, or better for the People with an initial capital, tend to be regrettably insensitive and arrogant to people as individuals.

A juggling word we can do without?

'Head teachers of the 208 most *prestigious* public schools', wrote *The Times* (shame!) in a prominent article in September 1975. *The Times* style book, that primer of conscious rectitude and correctitude, bans the word as a vogue word 'to be avoided at all times'.

What *prestigious* means, according to the *Oxford English Dictionary*, is: 'Practising juggling and legerdemain; cheating, deceptive, illusory.' The earliest recorded use, in a polemical Puritan tract of 1546, runs: 'Ashamed are not these *prestigious* Papists to utter it in their stories and read it in their Saints legends?' When the *Contemporary Review* of 1887 wrote of 'the grandiose language and the *prestigious* metaphors', it was not being complimentary about the metaphors.

Prestigious is going through a process of betterment, improving its meaning from 'tricky' to something like 'having or showing an illustrious name or reputation; endowed with prestige'. When the *Oxford English Dictionary Supplement* reaches the letter P in its magisterial retracing of its progress through the alphabet, it will be able to cite numerous twentieth-century uses of the word in its new white tie and tails of meaning; for example, Joseph Conrad: 'The *prestigious* or the desirable things of the earth craved for by predatory natures.' The latest dictionaries recognize the change in meaning that has taken place. The sixth edition of the *Concise Oxford Dictionary*, edited by John Sykes, the *prestigious* crossword puzzler, and published in the summer of 1976, gives the connexion with the modern sense of prestige as the adjective's only meaning, and puts the original connexion with conjuring tricks in brackets. The latest edition of Webster's, published in 1971, describes the primary, tricky meaning as archaic.

The change has been going on for longer than has yet been recognized by any dictionary; it contrived to escape even the eagle eyes of the original Oxford lexicographers. As long ago as 1819

D

J. G. Lockhart wrote: 'The *prestige* of *The Edinburgh Review* has now most undoubtedly vanished; but there still remains a shadow of it sufficient to invest its old conductors with a kind of authority over the minds of those who once were disposed to consider them infallible.' Lockhart was clearly using *prestige* in its new secondary meaning. He did, however, italicize it, which might suggest that he was aware of the strangeness of the usage. Almost certainly he was borrowing from the French in what is called a Gallicism. *Le Grand Dictionnaire Larousse* makes some remarkable comparisons between eighteenth- and nineteenth-century use of *prestige* and *prestigieux* by important French writers. They disclose an identical shift in meaning, except that the French words retain connotations of marvellous and amazing glamour from their disreputable past, when they were employed in taking white rabbits out of top hats.

All language is in a state of flux, based on the survival of the fittest. This is the natural condition of language: like other institutions it adapts to consumer demand. The dictionary can never, therefore, have the last word, unless it is defining a dead language. It is useless to bewail change, but useful to ask whether a change fulfils a purpose. How fit and how necessary is *prestigious*? Does it add a useful tool to the English vocabulary?

The original meaning of *prestige*, the unwed father of the illegitimate *prestigious*, is: 'An illusion, conjuring-trick, deception.' It came into English by way of French, from the Latin *praestigiae*, juggler's tricks. The quickness of the juggler's hand was able *praestringere oculos*: to blindfold or dazzle the eyes of his audience. During the nineteenth century *prestige* in English acquired its transferred secondary meaning of blinding or dazzling influence; 'magic', glamour; influence or reputation derived from previous character, achievements, or associations, or, especially, from past success. For those aware of its derivation *prestige* retains shady connotations, as if the reputation or influence is illusory and undeserved.

Prestigious is clearly a ragingly fashionable vogue word, intended to impress the reader with the learning and *prestige* of the man who uses it. Perhaps an age like ours that values *prestige* and PR more than merit needs the word *prestigious*, and can make good use of it. A large number of acceptable near-synonyms appear to be available: distinguished, eminent, reputable, important, remarkable, influential, and so on. With any luck the present fashion for *prestigious* will enjoy its brief fever, and then be seen to be otiose,

82

and so die. But when a new word is moving into the common currency of a language, to point out that it is being used to mean something other than its original meaning can be as profitless as trying to put out a forest fire with a soda siphon.

After the original version of this article appeared, Alfred Friendly, the distinguished and *prestigious* American journalist, wrote an agreeable letter to argue that none of the near-synonyms of *prestigious* were quite near enough. He defined the special meaning of *prestigious* as describing a person or institution whose pronouncements pack a special wallop, whose position enjoys a special importance or is safeguarded with a certain aura of repute.

He cited as an example Richard Scammon, America's best analyst of voting trends, who is distinguished, eminent, reputable, important, remarkable, and influential, but something more also: when he utters *ex cathedra,* you had better pay attention because he is *prestigious.* According to Mr Friendly, the Senior Wrangler at Cambridge and the President of the *Harvard Law Review* have *prestigious* posts, as they will happily find in the job market, where they are likely to do better than their contemporaries who have posts or degrees that are merely distinguished or remarkable. Harold Urey, the American research chemist who won the Nobel Prize for Chemistry in 1934, told Mr Friendly that a Nobel Prize winner could get away with murder, because his honour was *prestigious,* something different from and additional to all those other adjectives that are nearly synonymous. Linus Pauling can be described as a *prestigious* fellow; but his influence is rather less than he might like it to be, which may be a good thing. Alfred Friendly also turns his thumb down to 'distinguished', asserting that the word has been totally leeched of meaning in the United States by the deplorable necessity of every Senator having to apply it on the Senate floor to each of his ninety-nine colleagues, among whom are a significant number of stumblebums. 'Honourable' has suffered a similar devaluation in Britain because of the convention that Members of Parliament have to refer to each other in the Chamber as 'the honourable member'. *Prestigious* describes through the admiring eyes of others, without committing the describer to their admiration.

The battle against *prestigious* is probably lost. If it is accepted that *prestige* in its current and familiar transferred sense is here to stay, it is difficult now to shut the stable door against *prestigious.* Once a connotation for a noun is established, the demand will probably arise for a corresponding adjective; and language will, rightly, meet it. This process is not automatic. An adjective for 'integrity' would be a useful tool. But the correctly formed one, 'integer', has become obsolete except in its mathematical sense. The converse process of adjectives making corresponding nouns for themselves is also not automatic. For example, a noun for 'recent' would be useful. There is one, the useful and precise word 'recency'. But it is on the way to becoming obsolete because most people, wrongly, imagine it to be unrecognized by the dictionaries.

An interesting consequence of the current rage for *prestigious* may eventually be to anglicize and so shorten the pronunciation of the second syllable of *prestige*. The *OED* gives the anglicized pronunciation as an alternative, but it is never heard. Other words, like vestige, similarly derived from French have managed to drop their frenchified long last syllables. Perhaps we shall eventually say *prestidge*, which would be as cacophonous as *prestigious*. One of the reasons that *prestigious* may not last long in its new meaning is its nasty sound.

31 / RACE

Blurred colours in the immigrant tangle

The race relations industry has got itself into a tangle with its terminology because of euphemism and hypocrisy. Immigration legislation of the past fifteen years has been designed to restrict immigration from Asia, the West Indies, and other parts of what is politely called the New Commonwealth. The implicit purpose is racial discrimination. But this has not been admitted explicitly in black and white, partly in order not to hurt people's feelings, and partly for less honourable reasons.

Accordingly there has been a ludicrous search for an acceptable euphemism to describe what is being done, as silly as hunting a snark or a will-o'-the-wisp. Each new euphemism for racial discrimination rapidly becomes as explicit and offensive as its predecessors, and therefore has to be replaced.

There is a modern taboo, as irrational as most taboos, against talking about racial or cultural differences between people, and even admitting that they exist. The Victorian middle classes had a similar taboo against mentioning sex. We have a similar taboo against mentioning death. Mortuary words are becoming our unmentionables and inexpressibles, so that if we carry on at this rate the rudest expletive will soon be something like 'you putrefying old corpse'. Such strong taboos are always harmful to language, as in the tale of the foreign dinner guest, asked whether he wanted to wash his hands, who replied : 'No thank you; I washed them on the wall outside before I rang the doorbell.' Similar euphemistic taboo made the little girl tell her mother that her pony had gone to the bathroom outside the front door.

To get round the racial taboo the Home Office has introduced 'patrial' (intended as a loose synonym for white) and 'non-patrial' (non-white) into the language. But the definitions are exceedingly complicated, and the intended colours are not hard and fast. 'Immigrant' itself has come to be used as a synonym for a West Indian, or Asian, or African settled in the United Kingdom. This is as absurd as remote, xenophobic villagers who continue calling a new resident a foreigner, even after he has lived among them for fifty years.

Most 'immigrants' have been here for many years, and two out of every five of them were born in the United Kingdom. This euphemism produces such contradictory statements as the recent headlines in *The Times* that so many thousand immigrants were born in Britain last year, and that an 'immigrant visitor' has been allowed into the country.

Within the past decade, starting from the United States, Negro civil-rights militants have turned 'black' into a term of pride. Black has become politically a beautiful epithet for most West Indians in Britain. Many Asians do not like it, however, detecting derogatory connotations from the obsolete vocabulary of the Raj in the word; and judging that in any case it is an inaccurate description of, for example, Kashmiris.

The revolving cycle of euphemism has turned full circle in the United States: black has become acceptable, replacing Afro-American, which replaced Negro, which replaced coloured, which replaced darky, which in turn replaced black. Coloured is a flabby euphemism, and is considered contemptuous by those so described.

The latest silly extremity into which we have been forced by euphemism is 'non-white', as if the rude Anglo-Saxon natives were ever remotely white, instead of a muddy beige and pink. The use can just be supported by reference to white and black grapes, which are green and purple, or to white and black coffee. Non-white is a fatuous statisticians' word, but maybe it is the best that we can do.

In the present confusion it is probably wisest to spell out in detail what we mean, avoiding euphemism, as, for instance: West Indians, and Pakistanis, and Indians, and Bangladeshis, and Africans resident in the United Kingdom, and their descendants. This is such a mouthful that we need a more concise synonym.

The fundamental answer is not linguistic, but social: we should stop lumping together a large variety of disparate people and races, who have little in common except that the colour of their skins distinguishes them crudely from the majority of the population. But until that happy day comes, we shall occasionally still have to refer to people who are the victims of colour prejudice. Perhaps

86

'non-white racial (or ethnic) minority groups' is the most compendious and precise way of doing this, unless somebody has a better suggestion. But we should wince when we use the phrase, and reflect that it is a miserable society that creates such barbarous attitudes and such barbarous language.

Inflated treacle talk
and some fashionable false phrases

Advertisers, propagandists, and other stealthy persuaders use contranomers, or lying words that mean their opposites, as tools of their specious trades. Thus it is a safe bet that any state or organization that uses the words democracy or freedom, or their derivatives, in its formal title is an oligarchy or a tyranny. Some of the progressive education practised at the William Tyndale junior school in London seems to have been regressive to barbarism and anarchy. In this context 'progressive' appears to mean permissive, undisciplined, egoistical, and self-serviced. 'Progressive' is a chameleon word, changing its colour according to who is using it. It has become almost entirely a persuasive rather than a descriptive term. Virtually all proposals of all political parties can be described as progressive, and often are. What some brewers describe as 'special' bitter is in fact ordinary cooking draught. What seedy cinemas and pornographic publishers describe as 'adult' is in fact childishly prurient. Exclusive hotels and suburbs ought to mean places that allow nobody in. There is a hotel in the United States that advertises itself, with unconscious paradox, as the biggest exclusive hotel in the world.

Some of these dishonest words are merely comic or irritating to purists, depending on their temperaments. Others, however, are insidiously harmful over a long period, by brainwashing the public into false beliefs. *Reflation* is a good example of a false word used for euphemistic and propagandist purposes. According to its etymology and established usage by economists *reflation* ought to mean inflation undertaken after deflation to restore the previous position. *Reflation* is the first phase in the recovery from deflation and a slump, before the stage of full employment and inflation with rising prices is reached. But until now we have had little deflation for twenty-five years, because, in spite of deflationary measures from time to time, such measures have been more than neutralized by excessive government spending and the annual wage and salary increases.

The etymology of *reflation* is anomalous. The English language allows one to inflate or deflate, but not simply to flate a bicycle tyre. The economists have invented as tools of their arcane and inexact science both *reflation* and disinflation (mild deflation to curb inflation without precipitating abnormal unemployment), and given them quite specific meanings, in so far as any meanings in economics are quite specific.

However, dishonest demagogues and thoughtless economists and journalists have seized on *reflation* as a euphemism for inflation, which has a bad name. The suspicion is that when politicians talk about *reflation*, they are referring to something that would be correctly described in strict economic terminology as inflationary or even reinflationary. Political terminology is less scrupulous, and seeks to make the old process more palatable by removing the offending syllable 'in', and giving the old dog a new name. Such treacle talk gulls the rest of us into thinking that we can have continually increased wages and continually increased government spending, without the unpleasant concomitant of inflation. It sounds more comfortable if you call it *reflation*.

Industrial action is another very fashionable lying phrase. It actually means either going on strike, or working to rule, or going slow: that is to say, industrial inaction, or disruptive action. The falseness of this cant is increased when doctors, and other workers who have not the remotest connexion with industry, say that they are taking or threaten to take *industrial action*.

What they in fact mean is that they will stop or reduce doctoring their patients; which, in some cases, may do their patients a lot of good. Neither their spokesmen nor those interviewing their spokesmen seem to notice the ludicrous and contradictory incongruity of the phrase. Voltaire said that regimen and keeping fit were superior to medicine, especially as, from time immemorial, out of every hundred physicians, ninety-eight were charlatans. He would have approved of the charlatans downing stethoscopes. But he would have preferred them to call a stethoscope a stethoscope, and not an intracardial auscultatory interface.

Effete is a contranomer that is amusing rather than pernicious. Today it is usually applied to young men, when in its primary meaning it ought to be applied to women after the menopause. Its Latin derivation clearly proclaims its original meaning: some-

D*

thing that has brought forth young, hence worn out by bearing, exhausted, and often having ceased to bring forth offspring. From this the harmless adjective has come to be used figuratively in an intellectual sense, usually, for some reason, to describe men, meaning that they have exhausted their vigour and energy, and become incapable of efficient action, and dropping hints that they are homosexual.

33/ SCENARIO

Linguistic over-acting

Scenario is presently a favourite 'in' locution of swinging individuals who wish to maximize their on-going, high-profile conceptual postures speechwise in communication-type ambiances situation-wise. (That was not an easy or an agreeable sentence to get past a fastidious editor.) Like many other modern popularized technicalities it has been adopted from the theatre; and thence extended, distorted, and grossly overused. From the artificial glare of the footlights it has stepped down into the commonplace gloom of the auditorium in the footsteps of tragic, comic, dramatic, role, the two chief protagonists, and other showy histrionic predecessors. And like them, down there it often looks absurdly overdressed and stagy. We have it on good authority that all the world is a stage. But that is only one way of looking at the world. And role and *scenario* in particular impose on the language and our way of looking at the world an abstract, impersonal, and formalist version of social activity.

It was derived a century ago from the Italian *scena*, or scene; and its original and primary meaning is a skeleton libretto that preceded the actual work of the writing of the full libretto of an opera or play. It gives a sketch of the plot, the characters required, particulars of the scenes and a précis of each, the places where the principal dramatic and musical climaxes will occur, and so forth. After the *scenario* has been drawn up and settled, the details of the complete opera are filled in.

The anglicized adjective scenary, with the general meaning of theatrical or scenic, came into the language a century earlier, and has now grown obsolete: 'In the morning scenary diversions were exhibited', 1730. The German scenarium is a different thing. It means the complete libretto, with the full directions inserted for the scenery of each act.

Stevenson used *scenario* correctly as a metaphor, when in a letter

91

of 1880 to his publisher he promised to send him a full *scenario* (that is, synopsis) of his next book.

From these meanings came the use of *scenario* in a different sense by the cinema and television industries: the detailed directions and shooting-script for a film. And from this meaning, attractive to some because of the spurious glamour of the screen and the little box, an extended vogue meaning has been developed to indicate any projected sequence of events, course, or plan of action, especially one of several plans. It is especially popular in the military-diplomatic jargon of Defencespeak, for example in the language of war games, as an option or an account of a projected course of action or events. People speak of drawing up a number of possible *scenarios* in which nuclear weapons would be used. In British politics the word is increasingly used to mean a programme of action or merely a policy. In diplomatic talk we hear of the Security Council going through a complex but securely-plotted *scenario* to offer Peking the China seat. Space scientists fracture the language by considering fracture modes for various *scenarios* of mission failure. Amateur psychologists are said to pry into the mind of the rapist, to tune in on the obscene *scenarios* unreeling inside his head. And an alternative *scenario* is said to appeal to those Ministers who are said, equally mysteriously, to be sniffing eagerly in private for growth. Snuff was always supposed to stunt growth.

There is no fundamental objection to *scenario* being extended as a metaphor. The particular objection is that the metaphor is so recent and is still so covered in greasepaint and operatic costume, that in some contexts it sounds incongruous. Not all the world is an opera. Nor is all the world well compared with an opera. An opera about politicians dressed as hounds on the scent would need Aristophanes as script-writer to write the *scenario* to make it amusing. The second objection is that the excessive use of *scenario* is driving out older, more straightforward, less stagy words, such as plan, scheme, project, and so on.

One area where sexism is welcome

The Sex Discrimination Act, which came into effect at the beginning of 1976, has linguistic as well as social and legal implications. In certain circumstances it has become illegal to specify in advertisements the sex of candidates invited to apply for jobs. The English language, with its magnificently Protean flexibility, is quite capable of meeting this challenge without the whimsical convolutions around the theme of Madam Chairperson invented by mockers and even, it is said, by the zanier supporters of Women's Lib. 'Chairman' has long been used to mean a person of either sex; the phrase 'Madam Chairman' has been in common use since early in this century.

Nouns describing jobs, occupations, and vocations fall into three broad classes. First there is a large class that carries no semantic connotation of gender: for example, cook, clerk, councillor, motorist, nurse, teacher, and typist. In the case of the last, because in the past social custom has to some extent typecast typing as a female occupation, the scrupulous or meticulous advertiser can put 'either sex considered' or some such phrase in brackets after the vocation word.

The second class consists of feminine designations that either have been introduced into the language only recently, or have never caught on. Examples are editress, paintress, tailoress, doctress, and, perhaps, chairwoman. These present no problem, and will presumably now tend to fall even deeper into disuse. Nobody who understands English these days misunderstands doctors, or tailors, or painters, or editors, or, perhaps, chairmen to mean exclusively those of the male gender.

The third class is that of established feminine designations: for example, waitress, wardress, stewardess, actress, prophetess, duchess. If occasion requires the advertisement of one of these occupations, the advertiser, if other conditions make him (or her)

93

subject to the Act, must put in both male and female designations: 'duke or duchess required.' Or he must avoid sexual exclusiveness by turning the sentence around, as in: applicants of either sex are invited for a job in the police force, or as cabin staff for Concorde.

The richness and flexibility of a language depend upon the number of discriminations and shades of distinct meaning made possible by its vocabulary. The Sex Discrimination Act means that in a narrow range of circumstances the Queen's English must take second place to social justice, and give up some of its nice discriminations. This is socially desirable, but linguistically deplorable. It would be a pity altogether to lose such words as 'authoress'. It could conceivably be useful, for example, to say 'George Eliot, the authoress', in a context where her sex is relevant, in order to avoid misleading those who are ignorant that she was a woman. The prophetess Deborah is better than the prophet Deborah, because it distinguishes her in one short word from the common herd of Old Testament prophets.

For advertisements for jobs and products we can agree to give up or smudge some feminine designations, even though to do so makes the great word-fowler turn in his grave. Fowler argued that the way to make women equal was not to banish authoress as a degrading title, but to establish it on an honourable level with author; in the same way that actress is every bit as good as actor. Social practice rather than linguistic regulation will gradually and happily remove the adventitious masculine connotations from such vocation words as stockbroker, pilot, miner, and Prime Minister. Rapist will, for most conceivable occasions, retain its masculine flavour, though it is possible to imagine a female rapist with a Cleopatra grip. And the distinction between adulterer and adulteress may preserve some marginal usefulness.

But we must firmly resist other misguided attempts to emasculate or spay the language in the name of sexual equality. Much of the usefulness of a language consists in its thousands of discriminations. To reduce the number and scope of available discriminations, however worthy the purpose, is silly because it harms the language, and so diminishes us all, whatever our sex. Such nonsense as chairpersons, or the proscription of mankind (to be replaced by personkind?), or the invention of an artificial neuter singular pronoun to avoid having a masculine pronoun doing duty for both sexes is not just loony, but also mischievous. It is loony because, as the lawyers engagingly put it, in such cases the masculine embraces
94

the feminine. Man in English does duty for both *homo* and *vir* in Latin: man as opposed to rabbits and other animals, as in Homo sapiens; and man as opposed to woman. It is mischievous because it corrupts the language, and actually harms the cause of equality for women.

Sir John Adams suggested 'thir' as a sexless third person singular pronoun fifty years ago, and was disappointed not to find any supporters. But how many languages have a singular personal pronoun common to both sexes? In most contexts 'he' or 'him' can be understood to include 'she' or 'her'. If it is important to emphasize that both sexes are included in the pronoun, as it often is in advertisements for jobs, both pronouns can be put in on their first appearance: 'he or she will have a good degree and some experience of applied ergonomics.'

While the lunatic fringe of Women's Liberation strain at such semantic gnats as neuter pronouns, it swallows the whole male chauvinist camel of real injustice to women. The prejudiced, un-enlightened, and unjust are enabled to treat real injustice as if it were as trivial and silly as the fuss about chairpersons. We need to end the real injustice in jobs, and homes, and mortgages, and other aspects of life, and the language can look after itself. It usually does, rough-hew it how we will. Injustice exists in real life, not in dictionaries.

It is an engaging irony that the very word woman has a sexist bias in its etymology that would offend the more muddle-headed partisans of Women's Liberation, if they realized it. It came into English by way of Middle English *wimman*, from Old English *wīfman*, which literally meant wifeman. Most feminists insist with reason that just as one does not need to be a man to be a person, one does not need to be the wife of a man to be a person. As the next step backward down the brave but delusory road towards linguistic equality, shall we rename the movement Wopersons' Lib?

35/ SHRAPNEL

A highly explosive misuse

Civilians are notoriously imprecise in their deployment of military jargon. We take a noisy word with a whiff of gunpowder to it, and fire it off as indiscriminately as a blunderbuss, to overkill its original meaning. For example, all military men know a bomb, which is either dropped from an aircraft or rocket, fired from a mortar, or thrown as a hand grenade. And they know a shell, which is an explosive projectile fired from a rifled artillery piece, light, medium, or heavy. But who on earth ever bumps into a bombshell, except in a newspaper headline, where it means a shattering or devastating act or event? The blonde bombshell of the last war was an agreeable matriarch of this transferred use, neatly defined by the *OED Supplement* as 'a fair-haired person, especially a woman, of startling vitality or physique'. The distinction that a bombshell is always metaphorical, never explosive, is useful.

Shrapnel is a word that has been constantly misfired by journalists in their daily search for brevity and impressive technical terms, to the purple rage of some professional gunners. It takes its name from its eponymous inventor, Captain (later Lieutenant-General Sir) Henry *Shrapnel*, the nomenclator, and one of the choice and master gunners of the British Army.

Shrapnel invented a spherical case shot, which was tested on Shoeburyness Marshes from 1804 onwards. A picture of the screens against which it was fired still hangs in the office of the Superintendent of Experiments, Proof and Experimental Establishment, at Shoeburyness. *Shrapnel*'s shell was lethal because it was filled with musket balls. A small charge fired by a fuse opened the shell in flight, and the musket balls were propelled forward by the residual velocity of the projectile. The later invention of the breech-loading rifled gun and more accurate time fuses greatly improved the effect of the weapon, but its principle remained the same. The shell had to be burst in the air, and the balls pushed out of it by

96

a small charge of black powder. This explosion also made a puff of white smoke, so that the burst could be seen, and the next round adjusted as necessary.

Skilfully used, it was a very effective weapon against troops in the open before the 1914-18 war and in the very early battles of that world earthquake. The skill consisted of bursting the shell at the right height and range. *Shrapnel* was ineffective against troops dug in, unless the gunner was fortunately enough placed to be able to enfilade their trench: which means very fortunate indeed, in the way of the war for gunners. Accordingly, once the First World War had bogged down in the trenches, *shrapnel* was seldom used.

High-explosive shells can be fired to burst in the air before impact, when the fragments of shell casing have an effect somewhat like that of *shrapnel*. This tricky technique is called 'air-burst'. The traditional 'battle bowler' steel helmet of the British Army was originally called a *shrapnel* helmet. It was introduced to protect the wearer against *shrapnel* and air-burst HE, known familiarly as 'Jack Johnsons', or 'Black Marias' from the black TNT smoke they gave off. They caused many head injuries until the introduction of the *shrapnel* helmet, with its wide brim to deflect splinters. Its name suggests that the confusion between *shrapnel* and other forms of highly explosive death has been going on for a long time; in fact, since people stopped using *shrapnel*.

What journalists and other non-gunners call *shrapnel* today is in fact fragments from high explosive bombs or shells. The principle on which HE shells work is quite different: the lethal effect is caused by the fragments of the casing, torn apart by the explosion of the charge, and propelled outwards by it. Unlike *shrapnel*, HE shells are effective when burst on the ground, and do not call for anything like the same degree of skill from the gunner.

Shrapnel is now an obsolete weapon. In the Second World War it was used only against low-flying aircraft. So its erroneous or imprecise use does not greatly matter, except in so far as imprecision and error always matter. But when tempted to fire the word like a blunderbuss, spare a thought for the memory of Henry *Shrapnel*, and the professional susceptibilities of ancient gunners.

36/ SOPHISTICATED

*A sophisticated stance—
that's what it's all about*

In *An Essay on Human Understanding* (1690) John Locke wrote: 'Words in their primary significance stand for nothing but the ideas in the mind of him who uses them.' In *Alice through the Looking-Glass* Humpty-Dumpty in a rather scornful tone put the same idea more vividly and more succinctly: 'When *I* use a word it means just what I choose it to mean—neither more nor less.' Here follow a few fashionable looking-glass words that are changing their meanings:

Echelon: is a military term in English, meaning an arrowhead formation in which troops, ships, or aircraft are staggered, each with its front clear of the one in advance. The recent slipshod extension to describe any sort of graded organization, as in the upper *echelons* of management, is otiose (there are simpler words to do the job), and weakens the vocabulary by destroying the special meaning of *echelon.*

In French, from which English has taken *echelon,* the primary meaning of the word is 'the rung of a ladder', or, figuratively, 'each degree of a progressive sequence'. In the best ladders the rungs are set directly one beneath the other; and in French *échelon* would be a good metaphor for the higher ranks or rungs of management. In English it is acquiring the metaphorical meaning without ever having had the literal primary meaning of a rung. The *OED Supplement* gives examples of *echelon* in English from 1950 onwards (the first, appropriately, from that champion of portentous verbiage, Marshall McLuhan) of *echelon* being used to mean a grade or rank in any administration or profession.

Stance: means the position in which somebody is standing. Its ragingly fashionable extension is to mean attitude, view, or opinion. The new metaphorical use was vivid the first ten million times it was used. It has now become stale and boring, and is doing more precise words out of a job.

98

Sophisticated: is a lost cause. It comes from the ancient Greek Sophists, and used to be uncomplimentary, implying sophistry and artfulness. It has now become complimentary, particularly as applied to machinery, meaning up-to-date, complex, technologically advanced. In the scientific departments of universities it is used as a synonym for 'expensive', as in: 'My laboratory needs more *sophisticated* equipment.' When applied to persons, *sophisticated* has lost its pejorative sense, and simply means the opposite of naïve: a condition greatly favoured by modern society. It is absurd that this aberrant past participle, originally used to blame humans, should now be used to praise machines. But it has happened. At least we still have 'sophistical' available if we want to accuse somebody of sophistry.

That's what it's all about: a mindless bit of parrot jargon, much in vogue with sports commentators to describe some generally inconsequential fact that has little to do with the matter in hand. Even that fine writer, Anthony Burgess, questioned about the violence in *A Clockwork Orange*, replied: 'That's what life's all about, isn't it?', which was gibbberish. How the fashion started is obscure. The young giant in H. G. Wells's *Food of the Gods* kept asking, 'Wot's it all bloomin' well for?', when he looked down on London. A more probable and surprising originator is the late Iain Macleod, who said 'Politics is about the Centre'—a misstatement and an uncharacteristically sloppy piece of English, fit to father the present plague of other misbegotten *all abouts*.

Others ascribe the origin of the strange phrase to the old nursery dance called *Looby Loo*, of which one version of the last verse went:

> 'You put your whole self in,
> You put your whole self out,
> You shake it a little, a little,
> And turn yourself about.
> That's what it's all about.'

This was the original of the Hokey Cokey, a ludicrous dance that was popular during the 1940s in English dance halls. The last verse of the Hokey Cokey goes:

> 'You put your whole self in,
> You put your whole self out,
> You put your whole self in,
> And you shake it all about,
> You do the Hokey Cokey,

And you turn around,
That's what it's all about.'
It was the Cockney alternative to *Auld Lang Syne*, sung and danced at the end of parties. But there is a suspiciously long gap between those gaudy nights when they danced the Hokey Cokey in the 1940s, and the 1960s when *That's what it's all about* became a vogue phrase.

Whatever the origin, very few things or thoughts in this world are *all about* anything else. Perhaps people have forgotten how to emphasize particular facts to which they wish to draw attention. That may be what the odious smokescreen phrase is *all about*.

37/ STATISTIC

Blessed Fowler would not approve
of this statistic

According to the Blessed Fowler, slipshod extension is especially likely to occur when some accident gives currency among the uneducated to words of learned origin. *Statistic* is a current slipshod extension that would have provoked his formidable and witty disapproval.

The original version of this chapter asserted, intemperately, that *statistic* was a bogus singular. Borrowing the authority of the *OED* it asserted that *statistics* either was 1. (construed as a singular) the study concerned with the collection and arrangement of numerical facts or data, and inductive reasoning based on them; or were 2. (construed as a plural) numerical facts or data collected and classified. The article deplored the invention of a false singular, *statistic*, as unnecessary showing-off, and stated that all that the grandiose, fashionable phrase 'this *statistic*' usually means is 'this number' or 'this figure'.

Numerous eminent statisticians thereupon wrote, with some justice on their side, to cry 'foul'; though their letters would have been even more impressive if they had been unanimous instead of discordant in their definitions of the singular *statistic*. The weight of their exegesis came down that the singular *statistic* had led a blameless existence in their academic discipline of *statistics* for more than fifty years. It refers to the concepts behind the kind of numbers that statisticians are wont to discuss. For example, 'the average income of a sample of a hundred Oxford ratepayers' is a *statistic*—until it is actually calculated for a real sample. It is useful for statisticians to be able to distinguish between the general and the particular in this way. Of course, once you admit this word, you have acquired *statistics* as a genuine plural noun.

Their case for the singular *statistic* was put most authoritatively and engagingly by Mr A. W. F. Edwards, tutor at Gonville and Caius College, Cambridge. He explained that the modern use of

101

the word *statistic* in the singular derives from its technical use in the theory of *statistics*. In 1922, in a famous paper 'On the mathematical foundations of theoretical statistics', Sir Ronald Fisher, then a Research Fellow of Gonville and Caius and Statistician at Rothamsted, coined the word in the course of describing 'problems of estimation': 'These involve the choice of methods of calculating from a sample *statistical derivates,* or as we shall call them *statistics.*' Accordingly it is common, and proper, to refer to an average, or an index, or a correlation coefficient, calculated from a body of data, as a *statistic*. It is convenient to extend the usage to any single number which, by the nature of its derivation, cannot be but an estimate, such as the number of unemployed persons. Mr Edwards concluded that when he says of a quoted number 'that is an interesting *statistic*' he means (on reflection) 'that is an interesting number, though I doubt its exactitude'. It would be agreeable if the next edition of the *Concise Oxford Dictionary* were to give the definition: '*Statistic* (plural *statistics*)—a number of doubtful exactitude.'

All this is obviously potently true in the science of *statistics*. *Statistic* is the measure of a set or sample of numerical values. In this sense the weight of a baby at birth is not a *statistic*, but the average weight of babies at birth is.

Nevertheless, in the imperfect world of slipshod extension, away from the mathematical precision of statisticians, the singular *statistic* is misused ignorantly, often by journalists, as a synonym for a particular number or measure, instead of being correctly used to refer to the general. Its most notable vulgar misuse is to describe the bodily measurements of competitors in beauty contests. It seems to have emerged to offend the wider world at about the same time as 'parameter'. Journalists are probably the chief culprits for both errors. But their accomplices are social scientists, increasingly users and abusers of mathematics, who are not best known for their ability to separate jargon from the Queen's English.

Student needs more study

In our age that fusses inordinately about status, names of jobs are continually being euphemized, either in order to magnify the status of those who do the jobs, or, less frequently, to create a reason for paying them a little more. We all know how ratcatchers have come to be called rodent control officers, and dustmen, refuse transportation operatives. A pop song popularized by Lonnie Donegan in the 1960s would be translated by the official circumlocution of local or central government as: 'My geriatric head of family is a refuse transportation operative, what is your reaction to that? Make tick in the appropriate box.'

Newspapers do it too. Secretaries come to be called editorial assistants. The marbles reporter comes to be called the marbles correspondent, which is supposed to sound grander, and then Our Marbles Editor, although he is still doing what he has always done: writing about marbles. Generally there is no great harm in the nonsense. It does not lead to serious misunderstanding; and human vanity is a rich source of humour that adds to the gaiety of the nation.

However, the process can damage the language by devaluing old-established, precise words. This is happening to the noun *student*. *Student* generally means somebody who is engaged in or addicted to study. Its established secondary specialized meaning used to indicate a person undergoing a course of study and instruction at a university or other place of higher education or technical training. So a typical *student* of the old sort, male or female, was aged about twenty and working for a degree or diploma.

The word is now being extended in two directions. First, *student* is used as a dignified designation of anyone of any age who is having an education. The extension of the meaning started in the United States, where the distinctions between school, college, and

103

other forms of higher education are less clear than in the United Kingdom; and where the worship and flattery of the young by adults is more advanced. *Webster's* and the other American dictionaries apply *student* indifferently to somebody enrolled in a class or course in a school, college, or university.

The American extension has spread to the United Kingdom. So we now have primary school *students,* presumably studying for their BAs in Plasticine and finger-painting; the National Union of School *Students*; and graduation days for comprehensive school *students,* with no discernible academic degree for them to graduate in. Formerly people were schoolboys or schoolgirls until they became undergraduates. Presumably it is now considered age discrimination so to refer to them. But what is wrong with using the good old word pupil, instead of blunting the meaning of *student*? When everybody's somebody, then no one's anybody.

This first extension of *student* uses the word in a meliorative, adulatory sense. The second extension is pejorative. *Student* is used for any young person, generally foreign, who is doing something of which the writer disapproves: Dave Spart, a *student,* was charged with smuggling drugs. In such crimes *student* has become as loaded a term of disparagement as 'model' and 'company director'. Similarly the press report: in Ruritania a gang of *students* sacked the British Council library. All that they actually mean is the local rent-a-crowd of unemployed teenagers. What is wrong with the word 'youth', except for the sad impossibility these days of using 'maiden' as the feminine?

Research is another descriptive word from the terminology of education that is being grossly devalued by the tendency to flatter occupations, by giving them grander descriptions than they deserve. *Research* used to mean scientific study and critical investigation of new facts that were not known before, usually conducted in a laboratory or a library. Today the word is being used so indiscriminately, as a commendation, that a researcher is coming to mean no more than somebody who looks up a telephone number, or checks a few press cuttings.

It has been said of this new extended meaning, with as much melancholy truth as wit, that copying from one book is cheating; copying from two, a project; and copying from three or more, *research.* Heuristic methods of learning are popular and successful at all levels of education. The pupil remembers things that he has had to find out for himself more profoundly than things that

104

he has memorized like a parrot. But to describe such useful investigatory learning as *research* is to cheapen the word, which was originally and properly confined to the ability of somebody who had thoroughly assimilated a subject to create original material on it. *Research* is properly done by brighter postgraduates and their seniors, not by undergraduates and their juniors.

A chronic symptom not to be taken lightly

Syndrome is a newly popularized technicality, borrowed from medicine, like 'chronic', 'allergic', and 'hectic', and like them over-used and spoiled by misapplication. It is now widely used to impress the reader with the thought that the man who uses such a word must be a very superior person, at home with the latest developments in medicine and the cult of psychoanalysis; or, at any rate, with the latest fashionable jargon of medicine and Freudian English.

It is a Greek word, meaning literally 'a running together'. In classical Greek it was a rare word, used to mean a tumultuous concourse. Almost all the examples of its use in *Liddell and Scott* are from the Koine or vernacular of the Hellenistic and Roman periods, when the word was adopted by physicians such as Galen to mean a concurrence of symptoms: what doctors call the medical picture.

Modern doctors use it medically to describe a group of symptoms or malfunctions occurring together regularly, and thus constituting a disease or state of imbalance, either physical or mental, to which some particular name is given. For instance, Korsakoff's *syndrome* consists of a loss of appreciation of time and place, combined with talkativeness and other symptoms, forming signs of alcohol delirium. A *syndrome* is not itself a disease. 'He is suffering from an unfortunately antipathetic *syndrome* in his attitude to the new legislation' is a wrong use of the metaphor. Botanists use *syndrome* to describe certain plant diseases or disease symptoms, which are caused by a number of interacting factors. In modern Greek *syndrome* has diverged in another direction and acquired the meaning of 'assistance', with a specialized secondary meaning of 'subscription'. For example, in modern Greek transliterated *'syndrome ephemeridas'* is a subscription to a newspaper, not an ephemeral *syndrome*.

106

Over the past ten years, starting in the United States, the land of the brave and the home of the free extension of many other Freudian words, the use of *syndrome* has been widely extended to take in a great variety of non-medical conditions. There are ugly examples recorded of persons said to be suffering from a motor-cycle *syndrome,* on the insufficient grounds that they will carry on talking about their mechanical horses, in an industrialized version of the pathetic fallacy; and a private enterprise *syndrome,* because on assuming public office they forget that they are not managing their private firms. A word is said, truly and effectively, to possess a *syndrome* of meanings. A fine example of the use explains Albuquerque's allegedly all-enveloping friendliness as the Luke Short *syndrome*: 'Typically in a Luke Short novel, a cowboy, footsore and weary, comes into town carrying a saddle over his shoulders. Nobody asks any questions. Friendliness is simply his for the asking.' The *Economist* recently discovered, to make our flesh creep, 'a doom *syndrome*'.

The trouble is that *syndrome* is such a recent metaphor that its medical origins are not dead, but dormant. The word still reeks of the consulting room, and, especially, the psychiatrist's couch. If you use it in a grossly incongruous context, as in a physical fitness *syndrome,* or a football fan *syndrome,* you shock its medical origins to life again. If you write: 'Mr A. Politician, the Member of Parliament for West Woolgathering, is suffering from a Joan of Arc *syndrome* that may prove fatal', you run the risk of being taken literally, not metaphorically, and understood to be referring to disease and death. The wise man uses the word sparingly outside medical or near-medical contexts, possibly preferring some construction with the deader medical metaphor of symptoms.

Syndrome in English once, long ago, did have the non-medical meaning of a concurrence or set of concurrent things. Thus grandiloquent, magnificent Sir Thomas Browne, who never used a word of three syllables if he could find two equivalent periphrases of four, wrote of 'a *syndrome* and concourse of faculties'. And another seventeenth-century author wrote in a fine abusive phrase that deserves to be remembered: 'A Farraginous *Syndrome* of Knaves and Fools.' This non-medical use has been obsolete, but it is in danger of being resuscitated more horridly than Lazarus by the modern grave-robbers.

The original and scholarly pronunciation of the word is as a trisyllable, just as epitome is still, in spite of occasional lapses by the BBC, pronounced as four syllables. But the attraction of such analogies as hippodrome, aerodrome, and palindrome has proved irresistible. Accordingly *syndrome,* in addition to being most unethically abused as a non-medical metaphor, is now generally mispronounced as a disyllable. The mispronunciation has become correct.

Metaphysics and other academic questions are not to be trifled with

Politicians are the lads with a slogan on their lips, their tongues in our ears, and their faith in our patience. Many of the new words and metaphors that come into the language are coined by politicians. Politics are fertile compost for new idiom, from grass roots to bandwagons, and floating voters to the social contracts. Many of the new words and phrases are gloriously vivid when they are first used. Politicians are in business to persuade; and successful politicians tend to have a creative way with language. If they do not have the gift of the gab and a talent for popularization, they are in the wrong business.

Their most vivid and inventive creations are often widely vulgarized, and turned into vogue clichés. Everybody wants to play with the shiny new toy, and so its paint is soon worn off. Sometimes such political clichés are so grotesquely overused that they become a mockery and die of shame. Those two orotund old favourites of the political platform, 'to leave no stone unturned' and 'to explore every avenue', suffered that ignominious fate. Only the most inept, insensitive, and strong-stomached politician could bring himself to utter one of them today; and if such a man did let the phrase slip, he would run the risk of sniggers, groans, or snores from his audience.

Sir Harold Wilson, the former Prime Minister of the United Kingdom, has been one of the most inventive political word-makers, as befits the most successful British party politician of the past decade. Many of his phrases linger in the public memory: a week is a long time in politics; the pound in your pocket; that old white heat of the technological revolution (whatever happened to that?); and his sharp suggestion that backbench Labour Members of Parliament could be allowed one bite, but after that they might lose their dog licences. And think what Sir Harold did to popular-

109

ize to death such previously self-effacing adjectives as 'gritty' and 'abrasive'.

At least one of his new metaphors was deplorable, and is being quite widely adopted as a fashionable phrase. That is his use of *theology* and *theological* as terms of contempt, usually to describe the attitudes and activities of less pragmatic politicians in the Labour Party. The scorn in his voice when he dismissed such *theological* argument as worthless, and said, 'Let's forget the *theology,*' still echoes in the memory.

Of course, Sir Harold was not the first man to use *theology* as a contemptuous metaphor. There are examples of its being so used from the seventeenth century by men of letters hostile to religion, who considered *theology* to be 'nonsense's apology to sense'. And some of the more extravagant inquiries of old theologians invited contempt.

But this general new usage is deplorable both linguistically, and, if you will excuse the rude adverb, theologically. *Theology,* the science of things divine, may no longer be the queen of the sciences, compulsory for all university students, and boasting more professors than all other disciplines put together. But it is not a synonym for matæology, that is, vain or unprofitable discourse.

Even in a society that does not pay much attention to God, the questions that *theology* asks are still serious and relevant. What are we doing in the universe? Where are we going? How shall we live a good life? Good Heavens, they are even more important than political questions!

Sir Harold's misuse implies that God is dead, and that *theology* is exclusively concerned with such questions as how many angels can dance on the point of a needle. But a long and interesting correspondence in 1976 showed that not even the collective wisdom of readers of *The Times* could establish that any theologian, even Thomas Aquinas, has ever debated such a pointless question. Many modern theologians take the view that if *theology* is not about the market place and the rest of ordinary life, it is not true *theology.* The same could also be said about politics. Both sciences have things to say about ordinary life. Neither of them admits the exactitude of the physical sciences. The answers that recent politicians have offered for our predicament are not so overwhelmingly successful that it is absurd to listen to what non-politicians and even theologians have to say about it. It is arrogant, offensive, and erroneous to use *theology* as a synonym for rubbish.

There is a similar tendency among pragmatic politicians to use both 'metaphysical' and 'academic' as terms of abuse, to pour scorn on the more principled arguments of their opponents. The floccinaucinihilipilification (or habit of estimating as worthless) of metaphysics goes back at least as far as David Hume, who declared that if a statement were neither logical a priori truth nor empirical observation it should be committed to the flames as containing only sophistry and delusion. However, it would be an extreme and old-fashioned Logical Positivist attitude today to regard all metaphysics as a synonym for nonsense. Speculative inquiry that treats of ontology and the first principles of things, the ultimate science of being and knowing, may not produce simple answers. But, in the long run, they are quite as interesting and important as the everyday preoccupations of pragmatic politicians. Metaphysics is that which comes after physics (so named because it did so literally in the works of Aristotle), the latter being the study of nature in general. Thus the questions of metaphysics arise out of, but go beyond factual, or scientific, or even political questions about the world. And to use 'academic' as a derogatory term meaning coldly unpractical, abstract, and 'merely logical' is to betray ignorance of the purposes both of Plato's Academy and of scholarship generally, and also simple-minded credulity about the perfectibility of practical politics.

41 / TOOTH-COMB

Combing out the violent sporting clichés

Have you combed your teeth lately? Dentists recommend it for pyorrhoea and yellow fangs. And users of illogical cast-iron clichés increasingly use a *tooth-comb* for rigorous inspections that leave no stone or filling unturned, no avenue or cavity unexplored. It should be a fine-tooth comb, with its narrow, sharp teeth set close together. A fine-tooth comb is an old-fashioned implement to use in any circumstances. The vogue invention of a *tooth-comb* is a piece of nonsense that demonstrates how we slip into using absurd expressions by not listening to what we are saying, and not re-reading what we have written. So inveterate is the absurdity that the Oxford dictionaries, which are rightly descriptive of established current usage, rather than prescriptive of correct usage, now have to record *tooth-comb* as a figurative object. What an object!

While we are noticing extravagant absurdities, let us notice and animadvert on the vogue use of *reiterate* to mean to repeat. To iterate on its own means to repeat: to make, let us say, a charge, an assertion, or an objection repeatedly. To *reiterate* means to repeat all the rubbish twice or more times. Repeat is the workaday, exact word. *Reiterate* is a grander, inexact, and unnecessary word. Consequently pompous talkers and writers say *reiterate* when they mean repeat, because it sounds or looks more impressive. There may be contexts where *reiterate* is correct; but they will be only extremely rare contexts, when something has been repeated more than once.

Sporting jargon is a fertile seedbed for absurd extravagances that nobody could say or write in cold blood, if they considered for a moment what they were saying or writing. That is why the Olympic Games are tolerable on television only with the sound switched off. Gaudy sporting commentators tend to use violent hyperboles, such as massacre, annihilate, slay, smash, slaughter,

112

crucify, and thrash, when all that they actually mean is win or beat easily.

Consider these two splendid recent headlines from a sober and respectable newspaper: 'Irish can give underdogs added bite in their heroism of despair'; and 'Wolves enjoy taste of champagne after months of weak tea'. What apocalyptic visions are conjured up for the literal-minded by such extravagant sporting assertions? The answer is, of course, that one should approach sporting jargon with a pinch of salt and enthusiasm, not the vinegar of precision.

In our time we have all offended against precision when writing about sport. Most sport is exciting to play. Quite a lot of sport is exciting to watch, in the sweaty flesh or on the silenced box. But a blow-by-blow description of a sport is extremely boring for the average man who is not a fanatic or an expert. After you have said: 'Connors serves to the corner of the forehand court; Ashe returns down the line; Connors forehand volleys; Ashe backhand drives', and so on, twenty times, you have said it all; and the attention of the audience is likely to wander. There are only a very limited number of ways of saying that a batsman prods forward and misses, or that two boxers circle around each other pushing out their hands nervously and ducking and weaving. The temptation to enliven the writing or commentary to make it as exciting as the action is irresistible. That way lie hyperbole, occasional nonsense, occasional superb colour writing, and a good deal of innocent amusement for readers and listeners.

Arguably is a modish adverb in sporting and other discourse, which is being grossly overused, as if it were a synonym for 'perhaps' or 'possibly'. If a writer or commentator likes to think that Strider is a better centre forward (or jockey, or, for that matter, poet) than Clogger, then let him adduce his reasons. But who wants to argue about it? Most of us seem to take life in general and sport in particular more coolly than the professional commentators and scribes. We are prepared to discuss such burning questions amicably, but not to argue about them.

On-going is a transferred new recruit to sporting jargon, having been invented for those most dismal of sports, sociology and politics. It has now spread like the pox to pollute the sporting pages and broadcasts, usually in tandem with that other piece of waffle from sociologese, *situation*. There are few sentences that would not be improved by getting rid of *situation*; and none that would not be improved by getting rid of *on-going*, if necessary by

E   113 substituting 'continuing' for it. An occupational vice of sociology is to prefer pretentious abstract words to concrete simple ones. An occupational vice of writing about sports is to prefer violent metaphor and pretentious abstraction to plain unvarnished language.

Reds under the bed

We are getting ourselves into a muddle by loose use of *Trotskyite* and *Marxist* as indiscriminate denunciatory (or commendatory) blunderbusses instead of precise descriptive rifles. The proliferating sectaries and schismatics of the lunatic left squabble over differences of nomenclature and ideology so abstruse that sane men, who have other things to do with their lives, have no obligation to follow them into those deep and muddy waters. If one sect, for example, wishes to call itself officially the International *Trotskyite-Marxists* (as, doubtless, one does or will wish) then that is what we should call it, if we are unlucky enough to have cause to refer to it. But as general descriptive words we should try to preserve what discriminations survive in such strongly ideological and embattled terms.

Socialist has already been so widely and loosely extended that it has lost all precision that it ever had (not much, and with widely different connotations in different countries) and can mean as much or as little as democrat. Roy Jenkins, Sir Harold Wilson, and Eric Heffer all manage to describe themselves as *Socialists*.

Communist is a sharper word. It ought to be confined to members (official or crypto) of a *Communist* party; though there are, of course, considerable differences of doctrine and practice between different national *Communist* parties. Engels wrote, instructively, in his *Preface* of 1888, referring to the *Communist Manifesto* that he and Marx had written forty years before: 'We could not have called it a *Socialist* manifesto. In 1847 *Socialism* was a middle-class movement. *Communism* a working-class movement. *Socialism* was, on the continent at least, respectable; *Communism* was the very opposite.'

Marxist ought to be confined to a follower of the political and economic theories of Karl Marx: principally, those that labour is basic to wealth; that economic determinism governs human

115

activities in every sphere; and that historical development, following iron scientific laws determined by dialectical materialism, must lead to the violent overthrow of the capitalist class, and the taking over of the means of production by the proletariat.

Marxism-Leninism is the bureaucratic and idiosyncratic way that Marx's theories were altered and put into effect in the Soviet Union by Lenin; and one of the official descriptions by the Soviet Union of its political philosophy.

A *Trotskyite* or *Trotskyist* (*Trot*, engagingly, for short) ought to be reserved for a follower of the schism in Communism led by Leon Trotsky. Therefore, a true *Trot* ought to believe in worldwide revolution as opposed to '*Socialism* in one country', the attitude of national self-sufficiency and self-centredness that became Stalin's watchword in 1924. He should hold that historically the economic system has to be seen as a world system rather than a national one. He must believe that the economic development of every nation is affected by the laws of the world market, though such regional differences as resources and population make the rate of development different in each country. He must believe, therefore, that the permanent success of the Russian Revolution depends on successful revolutions in other countries, particularly in Western Europe. Behind the hyperbole of democratic rhetoric he must believe in the destruction of the mixed economy and the hegemony of the working class, because of its strategic position in industry, over the revolutionary and bureaucratic classes.

Of course, not everybody who calls himself or is called a *Marxist* or a *Trotskyite* subscribes to all (or any) of the relevant credos and shibboleths. The sects try to appropriate the mantles of authority from the eponymous saints of their religion, as Christian sects appropriate such validating epithets as 'catholic' and 'free' to demonstrate that they are the only true believers. Of course the doctrines of Marx and Trotsky have influenced the thinking of the British Labour Party and of most other institutions in our century. No less an authority than François Mauriac stated that 'Marx himself was a person in revolt against the world, but *Marxists* can no longer be such'. Those of us who care for the precision of the language, for the common good, should keep cool heads and take careful aim before firing such general epithets as *Marxist*. If used imprecisely as terms of abuse, they do the abused no harm, but harm the flexibility of the language.

116

43/ VALUE WORDS

Using the wrong tools for the job

The change from description to evaluation is one of the most potent agents for decaying meanings. Some words start life, like new tools, with precise primary meanings and sharp descriptive edges. Humans, in their propensity to exaggeration and careless-ness, use words that are meant to be descriptive chisels as evaluative screwdrivers. And, before you know where you are, you are left with a box full of blunt tools and a hazy vocabulary. Here follow a few chisels that are at present blunted and misused.

Democracy: No government has ever run successfully for long on a programme of continuous power to the people, which is what the etymology of the word implies. Direct *democracy* was practised, spasmodically and not well, by some of the city states of ancient Greece in the fifth century BC; but they managed only by not counting women, slaves, and immigrants as citizens.

Today tyrannical, dictatorial, and oligarchical regimes use *demo-cratic* republic and people's *democracy* as empty commenda-tory words of propaganda to mean 'better than the government next door, and if you try to go there to see for yourself, you will be shot'. Compare the use of 'freedom' to mean 'you would not like freedom if we let you have it, anyway'. The prison in Havana is called *Campo Liberdad,* a distortion of language worthy of Orwell's Newspeak.

Representative *democracy* in the liberal tradition of Western Europe, the British Commonwealth, and the United States of America is understood to mean open and free election of repre-sentatives, the possibility of dismissing a government, and other conditions that maintain the freedom of election and freedom of speech. *Democracy* in the people's *democracies* of Eastern Europe and the rest of the communist world does not admit the principles of the separation of powers, free elections, the rule of law, and the freedom of opinion, political argument, and association. These

117

socialist *democracies* mean by *democracy* popular power. By the powerful but increasingly imprecise word they understand the subordination of every interest and activity to the state, and the giving of precedence to the common good, by which they mean the good of the party.

These two opposed versions of *democracy*, in their extreme forms, now confront each other as rivals and enemies.

Communist, Fascist, Moderate, Radical, and so on: once sharp words used to describe the adherents of clearly defined political programmes, philosophies, or attitudes. Now generally used as ritual abuse of those with whose politics the speaker does not agree.

Legend: originally, a traditional but unauthentic or non-historical story. Now used to describe some person or organization having a special place in public esteem. The BBC recently described Caruso as 'a *legendary* figure'. When Sir Winston Churchill's cat died, it was described by the Peterborough column of the *Daily Telegraph* as 'a *legendary* figure'. BMW motor dealers invite potential customers, alarmingly, 'to drive a *legend*'. This vulgar misuse is too recent to have been noticed by the lexicographers, but the original offender appears to have been Lytton Strachey. In *Eminent Victorians* he described Florence Nightingale on adjacent pages as 'a living *legend* in her lifetime' and 'a living *legend* who flitted for a moment . . .'

This new use might be fancifully derived from the original meaning of the word: the story of the life of a saint, signifying exactly what the Latin *legenda* means, 'things designed to be read'. For example, the Italian Saint Bonaventure, the Franciscan theologian entitled 'doctor seraphicus', wrote the official biography of Saint Francis, *The Major Legend* (or Life) of *St Francis*, which was officially approved by the Franciscans in 1263. Three years later a general chapter at Paris decreed the destruction of all other *legends* of the saint. This medieval use of *legend* certainly did not have the modern connotation of being fictitious, though it presumably gradually acquired it from the zealous exaggerations of the monks, and the sceptical hostility of the Reformation to the traditions of the Roman Catholic Church.

The new meaning has come in as an exaggerated value word for somebody remarkable enough to be the subject of a *legend*; somebody who has a special status as a result of possessing or being held to possess extraordinary qualities that are usually

118

partly real and partly unreal, as in: 'a *legend* at forty-seven, as he has been for some years'.

Truth: originally, a concept with a number of associated meanings, complicated enough to occupy a wrangle of philosophers for a century. Now, little more than the official line uttered by that ubiquitous twentieth-century figure, Mr A. Spokesman, or 'an official spokesman'. When this article was first published it foolishly specified a particular sort of official spokesman in that last sentence, went into greater detail about what he did, and accordingly received a writ for libel. The sentence was intended as an epigrammatic way of putting the simple and self-evident *truth* that the double-talk of politicians, bureaucrats, and the rest of the public relations industry is often no better than half-*truths*; which are, of course, half-lies, or as Erskine May finds more acceptable, terminological inexactitudes. It was also one of the oldest jokes in the world.

Sir Henry Wotton, the Elizabethan and Jacobean diplomat, poet, and wit, made it in 1604 when he wrote in the album of Christopher Flechmore of Augsburg: 'An ambassador is an honest man sent to lie abroad for the good of his country.' It got him into hot water also. Gasper Scioppius, a Roman Catholic controversialist, used his contemptuous definition of an ambassador's function in a scurrilous book of abuse directed against James I and entitled *Ecclesiasticus*. James was not amused, and demanded an explanation. Wotton explained that it was intended 'but as a merriment'. But unfortunately he could not plead that the old pun on lying was there in his original version, because he had written that in Latin, in which *mentiri* can only mean 'to tell a falsehood': '*Legatus est vir bonus, peregre missus ad mentiendum Reipublicae causa.*' Wotton had been strongly in the running for the post of Secretary to the King. But a sense of humour is a dangerous quality in a statesman, making him at once suspect to those around him who take themselves seriously. Wotton's indiscreet joke ruined his career. He was in disgrace at court for two years, vainly trying to get official employment. Eventually he gave up the struggle, became a Member of Parliament, and retired to the back benches and the consolations of wit.

Truth is a dangerous value word; so is *good*. Note:
'Leave *Truth* to the police and us; we know the *Good*;
We build the Perfect City time shall never alter.'
(Auden, *Journey to a War*)

The man who uses tools for the wrong jobs reduces the efficiency of the carpentry shed for himself and everyone else.

Holocaust: originally, a total burnt-offering in which nothing was spared from the flames. Now, in journalism and other excitable prose, any fire that merits the attention of one or more fire engines.

Decimate: originally, to execute one in ten of mutinous, insubordinate, cowardly, or merely unsuccessful soldiers, to encourage the others. This was the main reason that the Roman legions tended to carry on fighting, while the opposition's virtue ran away to their legs. The new illiterate use has come to mean to destroy a considerable part of, to kill almost everybody, or even to exterminate completely. The most flagrant type of misuse is to say something like: 'They *decimated* almost half the enemy.'

INDEX

Canute or Cnut the Great (c. 995–1035), 16
car, 2
Carlos, 42
Carter, Jimmy, President and peanut farmer, 9
chairperson, 93–4
Chambers (lexicographers), xv
chameleon meanings, xiv, 88
charisma, 7–10
Charles, Prince of Wales (b. 1948), 36
Chasuble, Canon Frederick D. D. (1895), 38
Chaucer, Geoffrey (prob. 1345–1400), 1–2
Chauvin, Nicolas (1769–1821), 11–12
chauvinism, 11–12, 17, 73, 95
cheap, 2
Chetniks, 41
Churchill, Sir Winston (1874–1965), 118
Cicero, Marcus Tullius (106–43 B.C.), 22
claustrophobia, 47
Clegg, Walter (b. 1920), 70
Cleopatra grip, 94
Cleveland Street Scandal (1889), 35
clinical, 13–15
Clockwork Orange, A (1962), 99
Cloud-Cuckoo-Land, 16–18
Cocarde Tricolore, La, 12
Cogniard frères, 12
Coleridge, Samuel Taylor (1772–1834), 2
coloured, 26, 86
Communist Manifesto (1847), 115
communists, 115, 118
compound, 19–20
Comte, Auguste (1798–1857), 8
conic sections, 77
Conrad, Joseph (1857–1924), 81
consensus, 21–3
Conservatives, 22, 29–30
Contemporary Review, The (founded 1865), 81
Corinthians, 7
Corsica, 41
Cosa Nostra, 64
cosmetic, 24–5
Crockford's Clerical Directory (founded 1857), 71
Crofton, Sir Malby (b. 1923), 58

crystallography, 78
cute, 1

Daily News, 51
Dante Alighieri (1265–1321), 51
darky, 86
Deborah, prophetess, 94
decimate, 120
deflation, 88–9
de Gaulle, General Charles, 9
demagogy, 79–80
democracy, 117
deuteragonist, 15
devil and deep blue sea, 62
devil to pay, 61
Dickens, Charles (1812–70), 72
Dictionary of Historical Slang (Partridge), 34
Dictionary of Slang and Unconventional English (Partridge 1969), 59
Dictionary of the English Language (Johnson), xi
Dictionary of the Underworld (Partridge), 5
Dietrich, Marlene (b. 1902), 4
Dionysia, Great, 16
disinflation, 89
Disraeli, Benjamin (1804–81), 51, 80
doctors as charlatans, 89
Dolls, Mr Cleaver (1864–5), 72
Donegan, Lonnie, 103
Dorando Pietri, 76
Dutch, 45

echelon, 98
Economist, The (founded 1843), 107
Edinburgh Review, The (founded 1802), 82
Edwards, A. W. F., 101
effete, 89–90
ego, 47
Eliot, George (Mary Ann Cross *née* Evans 1819–80), 94
Elis, Peloponnesus, 73
Elizabeth II, Queen of United Kingdom (b. 1926), 36
Engels, Friedrich (1820–95), 115
English Perpendicular, 15
Erewhon (1872), 18
escalate, 19
Essay on Human Understanding, An (1690), 98
Establishment, the, 63–4
ethnic, 26–7, 87

Shakespeare, William (1564–1616), 1, 71, 74
Short, Luke, 107
Shrapnel, Lieutenant General Sir Henry (1761–1842), 96–7
Sicily, 17, 64
situation, ongoing, 113
Six Thousand Words (1976), xiv, 24
Skelton, John (1460?–1529), 74
skyjackers, 42
socialist, 115
sociology, 7–10, 113–4, and *passim*
Socrates, son of Sophroniscus (469–399 B.C.), 15
Sohm, Rudolph (1841–1917), 8
Sontag, Susan, 5
sophisticated, 28–9, 99
Sophists, 99
Sophocles son of Sophilus (c. 496–406 B.C.), 15
Sorensen, Theodore (Ted b. 1928), 58
Soviet Union, x, 50–2, 80, 116
Spanish, 41
Spark, Muriel, 2
Spart, Dave, 104
Sparta, 73
special bitter, 88
Speight, Johnny, 70
sport, 112–4
Stalin, Joseph (1879–1953), 116
stance, 30, 98
state, 51–2
statistics, 78, 86, 101–2
Steevens, George W. (1869–1900), 80
Stevenson, Robert Louis (1850–94), 46, 91–2
Stockhausen, Karlheinz (b. 1928), 78
Strachey, Giles Lytton (1880–1932), 118
Street Theatre, 42
student, 103–4
Suffolk dialect, 34
Sunday Times, The, 63
swimsuit, 2
Sykes, John, 81
syndrome, 106–7

taken aback, 62
television, 92
terrorist, 40–2
Teutonic English, 31

that's what it's all about, 99–100
theatre, 4, 14–15, 91–2
theology, 7, 10, 21–2, 109–10
Thessalonians, Epistles to the (c. A.D. 51), 7
Through the Looking-Glass (Alice 1872), 98
Timaeus of Tauromenium (c. 356–260 B.C.), 74
Times, The (est. 1785) xiii, xiv, 14, 32, 38, 51, 58, 68, 81, 85, 110
tooth-comb, 112
trauma, 47
Trent, Council of (1543–63), 21
Trotsky, Leon (1879–1940), 116
Trotskyites, 22, 115–6
truth, 119
tub, American tale of, 2

UNESCO, 77
United States of America, xi, xii, 1–3, 11, 26–7, 37–9, 52, 54, 58–9, 64, 79–80, 103–4, 107
United States Farmer-Labor Party, 37, 86
Urey, Harold Clayton (b. 1893), 83
Utopia (1516), 17–18, 69

Venus, Aphrodite daughter of Uranus or Jupiter, 32
vice, 72
vicious, 72
Voltaire, François Marie Arouet (1694–1778), 89

Wagner, (Wilhelm) Richard (1813–83), 65
Waterloo (1815), 12
Weaver, General James Baird (1833–1912), 80
Weber, Max (1864–1920), 8
Webster's Third New International Dictionary (1971), xiv, 24, 32, 81, 104
Wedgwood Benn, Anthony Neil (formerly Viscount Stansgate b. 1925), 79
Wellington, Duke of (1769–1852), 41
Wells, H. G. (1866–1946), 99
West Indian, xi, xii, 85–7
Wildeblood, Peter, 35
William Tyndale Junior School, 88
Williams, Kenneth (b. 1926), 4

126

Wilson, Sir Harold (b. 1916), xiv, 9, 49, 109–10, 115
Wodehouse, P. G. (1881–1975), 66
Women's Lib, 11–12, 93–5

Wooster, Bertie, 66
Wotton, Sir Henry (1568–1639), 119

Zeus son of Kronos, 17, 74